BREAKING THE CYCLE

OF INDIGNITY

WELFARE
REFORM
FACE-TO-FACE

Benetvision
355 East Ninth Street
Erie, PA 16503-1107

Phone: 814-459-5994   Fax: 814-459-8066
www.eriebenedictines.org
benetvision@eriebenedictines.org

Copyright 2002

No part of this publication may be reproduced in any manner
without prior permission of the publisher.

ISBN: 1-890890-12-X

02 03 04 05 06 07 6 5 4 3 2 1

BREAKING THE CYCLE OF INDIGNITY

WELFARE REFORM FACE-TO-FACE

This small book has been published to take a look at the real lives of some real people who have been affected by one of the greatest changes in United States social policy in 60 years. The stories presented here are true stories as told by welfare recipients in their own words. This book is an attempt to capture and preserve some initial efforts and the results of those efforts relative to welfare reform in the Commonwealth of Pennsylvania, and specifically welfare reform efforts in Pennsylvania's northwestern counties of Clarion, Crawford, Erie, Forest, Venango and Warren. This book is also presented to show the good will, stamina and the many challenges faced by individuals who are making heroic efforts to free their families from living on the edge of poverty. The book showcases stories of program participants enrolled in job training and placement programs at Saint Benedict Education Center headquartered in Erie, Pennsylvania. SBEC is under the direction of the Benedictine Sisters of Erie, Inc.

The names of the women and their families that appear in this book have been changed.

FOREWARD

by Miriam Mashank, OSB,

Executive Director, Saint Benedict Education Center

In mid-summer 1996 the United States Congress passed the Personal Responsibility and Work Opportunity Reconciliation Act (PRWORA). On August 22, 1996 President William Jefferson Clinton signed the Act into Law. The bipartisan support of the Congress for this Act and the President's signature initiated what may well be known as the most fundamental and dramatic social change in the United States in 60 years.

PRWORA replaced the existing entitlement welfare system known as Aid To Families With Dependent Children (AFDC) with a system named Temporary Assistance for Needy Families (TANF). TANF imposed a five-year lifetime limit for public assistance for 80% of all welfare recipients; 20% of recipients, defined as extreme hardship cases, were to be exempt from the five-year limit. The endless supply of federal money to the states was stopped; monies were to be delivered from the federal government to the states in the form of annual block grants. Once the block grants were depleted, there would be no more federal funding. For the first time in history, governors were given discretion by the federal government to carve out their own welfare programs and policies in line with directives issued by the federal government.

The welfare system (AFDC) inaugurated by President Franklin D. Roosevelt in the mid-1940s was designed as a federal entitlement program to assist needy families care for dependent children. It was an appropriate program at a right time for the right group of people. However, AFDC provided no incentive for a recipient to find employment and with the passing of time and changing societal needs and pressures, AFDC fostered a degree of dependency on governmental financial assistance on the part of some individuals. This dependency evidenced itself by becoming a style of life for certain individuals. In some families children grew up believing that public welfare was a way of life; they saw no role models among family members who inspired them to move toward economic independence. They, in turn, raised their families on public assistance. And so it was that for some families, generation after generation tended to become dependent upon public assistance for family subsistence for many years.

On March 3, 1997 the Commonwealth of Pennsylvania began implementation of federal welfare reform. Pennsylvania adopted a work-first model with opportunities for job training and education along with a number of supportive services for a two-year period. After that, welfare recipients are mandated to work at least 20 hours each week to continue with public assistance. Training and education options remain; supportive services remain. After five years of receiving welfare cash, cash ceases. Forever. Pennsylvania will, however, exempt 20% of the welfare population defined as extreme hardship cases from this loss of cash.

During the five-year temporary assistance period welfare recipients who, without good cause, fail to comply with Pennsylvania's welfare reform measures are subject to sanctioning measures issued by the Department of Public Welfare. Among these are removal of welfare cash from the potential principal wage earner for a thirty-day period after a first warning of non-compliance.

After a second warning of non-compliance, the principal wage earner can be sanctioned for 60 days. Food stamps and medical assistance remain in place as does cash for other family members. A third and final non-compliance warning may result in the entire family losing cash payments for a lifetime.

Saint Benedict Education Center, along with the Department of Public Welfare and local County Assistance Offices and with the encouragement of Erie County Executive, Judith M.

Lynch, and the Benedictine Sisters of Erie, Inc., has been a key player in implementing welfare reform in the Pennsylvania counties of Clarion, Crawford, Erie, Forest, Venango and Warren. The Center's case managers, academic staff, job readiness specialists, job developers, and support staff have worked with some 800 welfare recipients each year since 1996. Prior to that, Saint Benedict's staff worked with some 400 Erie County welfare recipients each year since 1989. The Center has strong financial support, technical assistance, and encouragement from Pennsylvania's Department of Public Welfare directed by Feather O. Houston, Secretary. Saint Benedict's has worked diligently to secure the support of local employers. That support has been forthcoming across the six county area. Employer support has resulted in Saint Benedict's job placement rate of close to 70% of those who terminate from our programs. The 70% figure becomes even more meaningful upon the realization that approximately 68% of the jobs carry medical benefits within a six-month period.

This book was compiled at the insistence of Anne Elizabeth (Betsy) Weiss, my executive assistant director. Betsy's creativity, competence, and never-say-die attitude, along with the entire Saint Benedict Education Center staff, have helped Saint Benedict Education Center become a strong beacon of hope for literally thousands who walk through our doors.

The Saint Benedict Education Center staff feels an urgency to move families from welfare to work. But not work that creates a new poor. The Center is not about reducing welfare rolls; it is about ensuring the social justice that assists families build a work history that leads, as quickly as possible, to moving them into a position of economic self-sufficiency. Welfare reform has happened. Poverty reform remains a priority item on the agenda.

YOU CANNOT HOPE
　　TO BUILD A BETTER WORLD
　　WITHOUT IMPROVING THE INDIVIDUALS.
TO THAT END
　　EACH OF US MUST WORK
　　FOR HIS OR HER OWN IMPROVEMENT,
AND AT THE SAME TIME
　　SHARE A GENERAL RESPONSIBILITY
　　FOR ALL HUMANITY,
OUR PARTICULAR DUTY BEING
　　TO AID THOSE TO WHOM
　　WE THINK WE CAN BE MOST USEFUL.

Marie Curie

INTRODUCTION
by Edwina Gateley

I have often pondered on what my life would have been like if I had been born and raised in different circumstances. If, for instance my mother drank all day instead of taking care of me; if poverty and abuse were my childhood realities instead of love and nurturing. No doubt about it, my life would have turned out very differently from the one I now enjoy, for I would not have entered adulthood sporting an impressive education and the luxury of actually choosing a career. Nor would I ever have imagined that I not only had the ability and the desire to succeed and do well in the world, but that I also had an inherent right to an honorable and secure place in that world.

The truth is that success in life (and by success I do not necessarily mean fame and fortune) is almost always built on childhood experience which provides the foundation on which we build our futures and our fortunes. The average person who holds down a job and brings up a family reasonably successfully, probably had parents who did much the same. This book is about adults who did not have such parents. It is about the dark, dysfunctional side of life which lurks behind the crumbling walls of poverty-stricken neighborhoods, usually hidden from our view as we get on with our acceptable and respectable lives.

This book does not tell us about respectable and acceptable lives. The poignant and painful stories told here remind us with startling force how blessed so many of us are and how deeply grateful we need to be for all that we have gratuitously received on life's journey. There, indeed, but for the grace of God, go I. What these stories present to us is a kaleidoscope of despair and dysfunction—a sorry catalogue of human frailty and misfortune where babies and children were reared without nurturing, affirmation or any sense of security. It is not surprising, therefore, that these children of chaos were yesterday's welfare recipients and, in recent years, became the first reluctant participants in the federal government's new welfare reform policies. Probably, for many, it was the first time in their lives that some level of achievement and success was expected of them.

Children from chaotic childhoods generally remain chaotic themselves unless radical measures are taken to surround them with new possibilities and opportunities. But, even more importantly, unless such practical measures as job training, education, social skills, child care facilities, medical help, etc. are also accompanied by compassionate support and understanding, lives will continue to fall apart. It is easy for those of us blessed with good parenting and childhood security to raise up our arms in disapproval when our sisters and brothers from the welfare system lose yet another minimum wage job or fail to turn up for that crucial interview.

What this book does for us is to leave us in awe that these courageous folks, with so much against them, even make it to second base in the first place! The fact that so many of them have made it to third and even home plate— is no less than miraculous! This book is as much about the endurance of the human spirit and the working of miracles as it is about the Welfare-to-Work Program. It goes way beyond the day-to-day struggles of students and clients en route to becoming workers and wage earners. It is a testimony to human courage in the face of dispiriting reality and enormous adversity; it is a testimony to what is possible when people come together with determination, commitment and hope to birth new life from despair. These stories are, for all of us, an antidote to the complacency and self-satisfaction which many of us feel in our middle-class, doing-very-well-thank-you lives and a shining tribute to the thousands of welfare recipients who have struggled so long and so hard to build new lives from nothing but their scraps of salvaged dreams.

We are left with a deeper awareness of connection to the individuals in these stories. A lingering sense of solidarity with their struggles leaves us standing like cheerleaders urging them on to success. We want them to make it. We applaud them when they do. We are saddened when they do not. But most of all, we hope for them. We hope for them because it is their due; it is their right, and an innate sense of justice tells us this. They have been deprived of enough. Now it is time. It is time for the human spirit to become what it is capable of becoming—free and proud and self-sufficient.

The hopes and dreams and successes in this book remind us of the words from Amos:

> *That day I will re-erect the tottering hut of David, make good the gaps in it, restore its ruins and rebuild it as it was in the days of old.... I mean to restore the fortunes of my people Israel; they will rebuild the ruined cities and live in them, plant vineyards and drink their wine, dig gardens and eat their produce....*
>
> Amos 9:11-14

POVERTY
MAKES YOU SAD
AS WELL AS WISE.

Bertold Brecht

ATISHA
by Holly Knight

A tisha looks like a cover girl. Sculpted with long, slender limbs, a graceful neck and a beautiful face with even features, she's got what fashion designers want. Given access to industry stylists, cosmetologists, trainers, and agents, she could earn five grand a day showing the latest seasonal collections on Manhattan catwalks—and make enough money to rent a posh Greenwich Village flat decorated like a spread out of *Metropolitan Home.*

Access is the key word. Who has it and who doesn't usually separates the residents of posh flats from the residents of urban projects. Without the privileges of access, Atisha doesn't drive home to an affluent New York address. She drives home to the projects in a rough neighborhood in the rust belt. Home is a tidy apartment sparsely furnished with a new TV her brother gave her for Christmas, a kitchen table with three chairs, two plaid love seats pushed against her living room walls. Her kids, Thomas, 5, and Brandy, 6, play on an old linoleum floor.

Born in Erie, Pennsylvania on April 5, 1979, Atisha was a wee two months old when her parents split up and her mother took her to Aliceville, Alabama. There in an isolated, segregated little town, located 10 to 20 miles from supermarkets, restaurants, malls, and the conveniences of contemporary living—without a car or buses or taxis—her mother and her three siblings shared a household with Atisha's great grandparents.

"My great grandparents were really old," Atisha, 22, recalls. "They'd just sit at home and do it the old way—live off of welfare, no job. My grandad, I guess he called it 'havin' a job'. He worked on cars and sold watermelons. Aliceville's not any place you'd want to live, that you'd think about settlin' down. People would just sit on the side of the street down there."

She attended Aliceville Elementary School, an all black school just like Aliceville Middle School and Aliceville High School. "White people stayed there," she says about the town's population, "but they went to their own private schools."

Around the age of eight or nine, her mother packed up and took Atisha and the brother closest to her in age to New York City. Her oldest and youngest brothers stayed behind.

"New York was big, amazing!" she remembers. "It was much better there. I had friends and we went skating and bowling. We had neighborhoods, streets, houses up on top of each other, stores right around the corner, buses, two cab companies, subways. It wasn't that far to go to the mall. Everything was right there, but it was too expensive."

They moved in with her grandmother (her mother's mother) and her aunt. In New York, Atisha's mother gave birth to a baby girl, a sister Atisha calls "her spoiled little self."

At the same time, Atisha's mother decided to face the ravages of the alcoholism she'd battled for years. With her mother in recovery, Atisha's grandmother stepped in to care for her and her siblings. Although her mother was on welfare, her grandmother worked in housekeeping at a New York hospital, and showed the kids a different way of life.

"When my grandmother was takin' care of us, we was goin' to church, and I was doin' good in school. I was a good little girl then," she says.

But their New York residency was short-lived—three, maybe four years. While her mother remained in New York, she sent Atisha and her brother back to Alabama to live with her great-grandparents again.

"That's when I got wild down there," she admits, "'cause my grandmother let me do anything I wanted. We helped her do whatever she wanted, and we ate good, but she was a mean person. She had little names for us. My name was 'Pissy' and my brother's name was 'Blacky.' My other two brothers, those were her favorites. They stayed with her all the time. They're still with her."

She put in a dismal academic performance that she mostly blames on hanging out with friends who drank, smoked and regularly skipped school.

During that stint in Alabama, Atisha, at 14, got pregnant.

"I really didn't know," she recalls. "I mean, I was missin' my period, but I was a young person and I was happy it wasn't comin'. I wasn't thinkin' that I was pregnant 'cause really no one had ever sat down and talked to me about the birds and the bees."

It wasn't until she traveled up to Erie to attend her father's funeral that her grandmother noticed Atisha was showing. She was probably four or five months along when her grandmother confronted her and made her see a doctor.

She delivered her daughter, Brandy, in Erie on March 26, 1994, a few weeks before her fifteenth birthday. Two months later, she discovered something wrong with the baby's breathing. Doctors diagnosed her with one paralyzed lung and the other lung malfunctioning.

Brandy required immediate surgery, but the Erie hospitals weren't equipped for such intricate operations on infants. So Atisha accompanied little Brandy in an ambulance all the way to Children's Hospital in Pittsburgh, where doctors performed surgery and a tracheostomy.

"I was in the eighth grade," Atisha recalls. "I was on the honor roll. I finished the eighth grade, but I had to quit goin' to school to take care of Brandy." Atisha stayed with her daughter day and night during the intensive care period following surgery—about two weeks—and remained by her bedside throughout her six-week hospitalization. Atisha's mother joined them. The nurses taught her the procedure for taking care of the tracheostomy during her daughter's recuperation.

Before doctors removed the tracheostomy, Atisha's

mother took them back to Alabama. Brandy was three or four months old.

"I started to go back to school down there, but my grandmother didn't know the procedure for takin' care of the tracheostomy," Atisha says. "My mom did, but she was drinkin' then. So I was the only one who could take care of her."

The procedure required removing the tube from the baby's neck, cleansing the incision area, suctioning out the opening in her neck and replacing the old tracheal tube with a new one. "It was hard 'cause you couldn't hear her cry," Atisha remembers. "All you could hear was that phlegm that would be in her neck. But thank God they finally took the tube out within six months."

During that sojourn in Alabama, Atisha got pregnant. "I did everything I could to have a miscarriage," she says, "but everything I tried didn't work." Before she delivered her son Thomas, her mother and brothers left Alabama and headed back up North, leaving Atisha and Brandy with her grandparents.

"One day I called my grandmother a liar," Atisha says. "She hit me on top the head with a butcher knife and sent me to a maternity home in Mobile. They put my daughter in a foster home. I stayed in the maternity home until I had my son, then they put us in a foster home, too. We were there two or three weeks. Then I moved back with my grandmother and I got my daughter back. That's when we moved to New York and stayed with my grandmother and aunt.

"But I hated goin' from this place to that place," she says. "Leavin' friends here, leavin' friends there. We just did so much movin', it was outrageous!"

The weight of Atisha's responsibilities grew heavy. Her one-time vision of what life would be like for her unraveled.

"It was horrible," she says. "Everybody said, 'You ain't never gonna finish school. You ain't never gonna do this or that. You ain't never gonna accomplish anything 'cause you got kids. They're gonna always hold you back. You ain't never gonna have nothin'.'"

Atisha admits she was too young and immature to think about planning any kind of direction for herself then and says she didn't start to grow up until she was 17 or 18, when she realized she had to make her own life.

"In New York it was real hard for me," she says, "'cause I was a single mom. I was stayin' with my grandmother and my aunt. My mom went into rehab. I was on welfare at the time. They was payin' for my rent. I got $97 every two weeks. I wasn't gettin' no food stamps 'cause I was stayin' with my grandmother. She was workin' in the hospital in housekeeping, and they was goin' from her income. So I didn't get no food stamps. I was 18—old enough to get welfare but not food stamps!"

They shared three bedrooms and paid $700 a month for rent. But not long after Atisha's arrival, the landlord died. The landlord who took over raised the rent to $900.

Atisha's frustration intensified.

"For me to go out and get a job, it was hard," she says. "My mom got out of rehab and was doin' good. She was workin'. My grandmother was workin'. Everybody was workin'. It wasn't like I could do anything 'cause I didn't have a babysitter."

Atisha wanted to go out on her own, but she knew New York was too expensive to make it possible. Since her brother lived in Erie, she called him and asked if she and the kids could come up. She figured the cost of living in Erie might enable her to get her life together.

"So I moved up and got on welfare," she explains. "Then things went bad with me and my brother. He kicked us out. That's when I went to the shelter on 26th Street. We stayed there for almost a month. That's when I got me a crib. I was goin' to school at St. Ben's (Saint Benedict Education Center) for gettin' my GED (Graduate Equivalency Degree). Welfare here makes you do somethin', so I just chose St. Ben's 'cause it was the closest."

Lucky for her. St. Ben's is not a job mill. Although self-sufficiency is the center's goal, the staff does as much with self-esteem as they do with books; and their first focus is to convince their clients they can learn. And Atisha learned.

Soon after she earned her GED, she got a job. Supportive Living Services hired her as a human services associate, a position that pays her $8.63 an hour or roughly $16,600 annually. They placed her in group homes where she works with mentally and physically disabled people, helping them prepare and cook meals, shop for groceries, get ready for bed, go on outings and socialize with each other.

Although Supportive Living Services provides health insurance for Atisha, they don't cover her kids. She must still rely on Medicaid to cover Brandy and Thomas's medical expenses. "I have a wonderful job," she said on more than one occasion and considers her-self much better off now. Mid-summer and again next fall, she'll be up for raises.

After she earned the GED, learned how to drive, got her driver's license, and the job, St. Ben's got her a car. A few months later she applied and qualified as one of 15 people accepted into a new lease-to-purchase housing program. Sometime soon, Atisha and her kids will move into a two-story, three-bedroom house with a bath and a half and a detached garage. The house is one of 15 being constructed by Erie's Housing and Neighborhood Development Service (HANDS), a non-profit agency providing affordable homes in a mid-town section of the city. For her part, Atisha, like all the new HANDS residents, must participate in neighborhood watch groups and receive home ownership and financial counseling. The new homes and increased police protection in the mid-town neighborhood are part of a community strategy to clean up the neighborhood, which still appears to fall into the same red-lined community Atisha lives in now. Frequented by prostitutes and crack dealers, the absence of supermarkets and banks is glaringly obvious. A run-down business district with mostly boarded up storefronts lines Parade Street, the main drag, located a block or two from the HANDS homes. Erie County Prison sits only blocks away. Access remains elusive.

Earning her GED, landing a job, getting a driver's license, owning a car and being selected for home ownership—all within a year—provided Atisha with a windfall of tools and assets upon which to build the foundation of her and her kids' lives—a foundation that barely existed a year ago. Those accomplishments garnered another kind of asset. In April of 2000, she won a Governor's Achievement Award, a distinction that recognizes what the strength of grit, the love of kids and a recovering self-esteem can do. The award also came with two citations—one from Pennsylvania's House of Representatives and the other from the Senate, commending her for her "extraordinary and enduring human spirit." Because of these three affirmations, Atisha can now envision a future where none existed in the past.

* * *

By the time I met Atisha, in September of 1999, the GED, driver's license, car and job offer were achievements already in hand. I knew little about her except what I heard in a brief summary about her nomadic childhood. Given the unstable circumstances she'd faced, I expected to meet somebody with a hard edge, somebody with a noticeable chip on her shoulder, somebody who might not want to look me in the eye or who'd resent me for my white privilege.

But her demeanor was warm, a bit reserved but forthright, cautious but cooperative. I knew she was a reluctant participant in this project: she'd only agree to participate if I would meet her condition: She wanted to read her story before I turned it over to be published. Educated and trained as a journalist, that's a line I fiercely protect, knowing censorship usually crimps a journalist's freedom to write an honest story. I hesitated, but reluctantly agreed. So I guess we shared equal ground.

Atisha works the late-afternoon until late-night shift, from about 3:00 p.m. or 4:00 p.m. until midnight, five days a week. She gets Wednesdays and Thursdays off, which we decided to use for interviews. Because neutral ground seemed like the best place to start, we agreed to meet at St. Ben's. We met for the first interview, but she showed up too late to conduct a complete interview the next few weeks; then she canceled one and didn't show up at all for the following interview. Just when I felt like throwing in the towel, she called and apologized. At her social worker's suggestion, I asked Atisha if we could just meet at her place instead of at St. Ben's. "All you have to do is be there," I said.

Opening a door to a stranger takes some trust. When she accepted the suggestion, she opened a new level of her life to me.

No window faces the entry to Atisha's place. Just a solid door with a peep hole at the top. Each time I arrived and knocked on the door, Thomas and Brandy screened me.

"Who is it?" they'd shout.

"It's Holly."

"Who?"

"It's Holly to see your mom."

"It's Holly," I heard them echo.

Several seconds later, the kids opened the door.

Sometimes Thomas ran over and hugged me. Sometimes the kids just looked at me and asked why I was there. "I'm writing a story about your mother," I'd remind them. They never pursued it any further. Who knows what they thought? Maybe so many social workers and red-tapists come to scrutinize them, they figured that writing someone's story just meant another bureaucrat sizing them up.

Atisha never answered the door. Most of the time the kids got her out of bed. While I waited, the kids and I talked. One afternoon Thomas excitedly ran into the back and brought out a new pair of sneakers to show me. Cool shoes. Great colors. Brandy followed suit, fetching her more feminine pair.

Sometimes Brandy wanted to talk about what she learned in kindergarten. On one occasion she brought me a sheet of paper with drawings she'd composed. The pictures illustrated words typed on the paper—bird, sun, house, flower. Brandy interpreted each rendering like a docent in an art museum.

I looked at my watch. It was 12:30.

"Why aren't you in school today?" I asked.

"Because my mom was sleepin'," she replied.

After Atisha got up and cleaned off the kitchen table, we sat down and began our interview. We got through the topic for the day, so I asked her about Brandy missing school.

"Yeah, sometimes I just sleep in and by the time I wake up it's too late to take her to school. I know I should get up, but sometimes I'm stayin' up till 4:00 a.m. hangin' with my friends," she said.

The thought that Brandy's young thirst to learn took second place to Atisha's social life disturbed and saddened me. I wanted to start driving over during my lunch hour to make sure Brandy got to school everyday. But my second thoughts were wiser. Realizing that I would just be supporting Atisha's night life, I wisely thought better of that idea.

Atisha grew up in isolation, segregation and urban overpopulation. She was reared by role models who carried the weight of more than their share of handed-down hardships. She left behind her future to take up her responsibility as a mother when she was in the eighth grade. Transformation isn't usually a flip-of-a-switch occurrence. Its natural pace is slow and often erratic.

This is a very short story, a tiny time capsule packed with some monumental change. In this singular life I see the trail of struggles common to many poor African-Americans still trying to break the spell of the one-step-up-and-two-steps-back rhythm of racism and rights. Atisha's life embodies that tension—the tension of this country's most despicable social legacy and the fragile hope of a new, more equitable, just and liberating era struggling to be born.

Although I didn't count the number of times she repeated the phrase, "It was hard," I heard the mantra often enough throughout her recollections to notice the implications.

"It was hard" comes from deep suffering. "It was hard" comes from hitting wall after wall with no options. "It was hard" comes from the gut-wrenching emptiness of dumping all your dreams in exchange for minimal survival skills. "It was hard" comes from living a life within "a climate of no accountedness," to borrow the words of African-American minister, mystic and prophet Howard Thurman.

"It was hard" doesn't emerge in a social vacuum. It emerges from the foundational factors that formed Atisha's self-identity. Family instability, poverty, segregation, social and institutional injustice don't just describe external conditions. They breed internal degradation. They undermine self-esteem, cut off the roots of self-confidence, generate self-hatred, anger, frustration, instability and despair.

Now, as Atisha walks away from the welfare rolls and walks into the workforce, I see a passage with more questions than answers. Does she have a career path that will enable her to move up the rungs of the economic ladder? Will her children receive a viable education that will provide them with the same opportunities, dignity, authentic empowerment and access to privileges most Americans take for granted? Can the shackles that bound Atisha's developmental years be broken to free her from the constriction of hardened survival skills?

Looking back at the changes in her life over the past year, Atisha shares what motivates her to keep building on her successes. "I got to look out for my kids. If I don't, nobody else will," she says. "I had a rough life when I was little. I don't want the same for my kids. I want to get them things and I want to get my house situated, but I got to wait. I go out and party, but I also take care of my priorities—such as my kids, my bills, food in the house, buying my kids clothes. You know it ain't been that easy as far as getting' them things right away. But everything is centered on my kids and my house."

The Welfare Reform Act is asking its former recipients to face a colossal challenge: make a total transformation and, by the way, you have a deadline. The Governor's Achievement Award might be a good way to start rewarding the welfare poor for moving off its rolls, but the real pay off will come when the welfare poor can move out of the ranks of the working poor.

Atisha may not bring home five grand a day modeling on Manhattan catwalks, but what she's modeling for her two young children is the heroic conquest of some of the most formidable obstacles society constructed to confine her.

THE TROUBLE
WITH BEING POOR
IS THAT
IT TAKES UP
ALL YOUR TIME.

Willem De Kooning

THE PHOENIX PROGRAM
by Julie Cullen

E ven under the best of circumstances, the trial of rising out of poverty is an almost insurmountable task. The move from welfare roles into the workforce is marked by drastic personal changes and social pressures. Additionally, the stigma of welfare that imprints itself onto the person receiving assistance must be overcome. Now, pressure from new legislation limiting assistance and the amount of time each person is allowed to receive benefits adds to the burden that must be carried. This country has always counted as heroes those among us with the courage to try what the rest of the world considers impossible, to remake themselves and rise from their past as a phoenix from its own ashes. Today, as Nikisha prepares for a future without assistance, a new kind of survivor emerges.

This story begins at the crossroads of one woman's life. For Nikisha, the decision to begin receiving assistance was made not because it would be the easy road, but because it was the only road to take. Life had not left her many choices. As the mother of two young children, Nikisha was determined to provide for them the very best life she could possibly manage. Facing an unsure future, she decided to find some new way to improve her life. With the support of her family and strength from her faith, Nikisha applied for assistance. Welfare not only provided the monetary and food assistance that Nikisha needed for herself and her children, but it also provided the opportunities that could make the difference between just working and succeeding.

Coming from a family that values education and hard work, Nikisha believes that you get out of life what you put into it. Nikisha's grandmother could boast to her neighbors that all of her children and grandchildren have high school diplomas. Strong-willed and determined parents and grand-parents would accept nothing less from Nikisha, her siblings, and cousins. Education is viewed in her family as the path to the brightest future. When her children were born, Nikisha saw welfare as something that would be a short-term help. She wanted to get things established for her children, then return to work. For years Nikisha worked in restaurants, as a cashier, as a court reporter, and at other jobs that did not require extensive training or education. With two kids, her own education had to take a back seat to their needs. None-theless, Nikisha always wanted to get the kind of training that would help her to get a job in an office, somewhere professional, with room to move up and ultimately give her children a better life. The new laws for welfare were a mixed blessing; although there was a limited length of time she would be allowed assistance, it would provide her with the training she wanted.

For someone who had worked since high school, it was a difficult decision to receive assistance, but Nikisha believed it would be the path to a brighter future.

Nikisha entered Saint Benedict Education Center (SBEC) in a five-month "Up-Front" program designed to be an academic brushup, provide job readiness preparation and job placement assistance. The transition into the program was not easy. Nikisha had to learn to juggle the full-time responsibility of raising two kids, the stresses of her own personal life, and the demands of her training. She had to learn to bear the pressure of the looming deadline. She had to overcome the nagging self-doubt that she might not be able to get the kind of job and the kind of life she wanted, no matter how much training she had. She had to cope with the fact that she no longer had her own paycheck. She had to manage the stress of making a minimum amount of money, less than the $700 a month that the United States government provides through welfare, and stretch it to cover the needs of three people.

During the first few months of the program Nikisha absorbed everything. She was able to survive the weight of her challenges and fears, and tried to learn as much as she could. Her drive and determination were recognized and encouraged by her teachers. Nikisha found support and understanding from veteran teachers who were familiar with many of the trials people in their programs were facing. As Nikisha progressed through the program, she began to shed the fears that might hold her back. She grew more and more confident, knowing that if she just had enough time to develop the skills she hoped to learn she would be able to get into the job market and do the sort of work she wanted. She needed more time. Nikisha confided to her teachers her fear that she was unprepared, that she did not feel ready to try for the kind of job that she wanted. With the support and guidance from the SBEC staff with whom she was working, Nikisha was able to enroll in the Single Point of Contact [SPOC] program.

SPOC is designed to ensure that needs are met to help a person rise out of poverty through employment. The program helps participants get their GED if they do not have a high school diploma and receive additional training for up to a year. Career and job counseling, job placement, support for child care, transportation, and personal needs are also included for participants in the program. SPOC provided Nikisha with a real possibility for achieving her goals. The pressure of being under time limitations was momentarily lifted. During the yearlong program, she received instruction in bookkeeping, medical and legal terminology, health and wellness education, and English composition. She was trained to use faxes, phone systems and copiers, and mastered other clerical skills. She learned computer skills including word processing, spread sheets, data processing, desktop publishing, and specialized presentation programs such as *Power Point*.

Nikisha was always quick to volunteer to help anyone learn concepts on the computer or with anything else they needed. Midway through her program, Nikisha was asked by her computer instructor to give a presentation to the incoming students of the SBEC programs, the executive director of the program, and an official from Harrisburg. Cool under pressure, Nikisha explained to the group what each instructor would teach and what to expect from the process. With precision and clarity, she talked about job counselors and job placement personnel. She gave the new students a pep talk, explaining that they would get out of the program only what they put into it. Her energy and passion for education transformed the room. Nikisha dazzled the group and made their immediate transition, so difficult for most new students, much easier to anticipate.

Nikisha's computer instructor was thrilled with her performance. She remarked that Nikisha could learn as fast as she could teach, and all she needed was time to gain experience. To force Nikisha into a job without giving her the extra training would undermine everything that the welfare program is trying to accomplish. Welfare is not a permanent solution to poverty, but there needs to be a balance between not allowing people to make welfare a way of life and issuing a premature deadline to move someone into the workforce. Without extending Nikisha's assistance, she may have been eliminated from programs that would allow her to realize her full potential. As she moved through the program, Nikisha became less paralyzed by her fears, more willing to stand up for herself, and helpful to anyone who needed her.

In the middle of her training, personal tragedy struck. One of Nikisha's family members was murdered. The press sensationalized the murder as a drug deal gone bad, although her cousin had never been involved with drugs or the drug lifestyle. The young man was simply in the wrong place at the wrong time, making the tragedy all the more difficult for his family to accept. It was a roller coaster of emotions for Nikisha and her family. The family was not only faced with the loss of their beloved Nick, but they also had to learn to cope with the murder and the future trial of the killers, as well as the relentless pursuit of the press. Nikisha felt responsible to her family in helping them cope with the loss. She tried to help coordinate information coming from the District Attorney's office and to help her family not only respond to inquiries from the press, but also to react to the publicity surrounding the death. The pressure of the situation, her own grief, and her struggles with the demands from the program at SBEC almost caused Nikisha to quit. She started to feel as if all of these pressures had backed her into a corner so tightly that she could barely breathe. The loss has affected every aspect of her life. She still struggles through her grief and her shaken sense of security. Most difficult of all, Nikisha must overcome the pain and confusion and help guide her children through their questions about death and violence. Nikisha believes that it was only with the support of the staff at SBEC and her friends, the strength of her family, and her belief in God, that she was able to continue toward her goals.

Nikisha never quit. She may have been tempted, but she stayed focused on her goal. Nikisha wants a good job, a good home and a backyard where her kids can play. She lives two blocks from where she grew up in a housing project on Erie's east side. From her window, she watches her kids play on the same street she and her friends used to roam. She remembers practicing dance routines in homemade costumes for a community talent competition and regrets that her children have to be concerned with drug dealers and violence. What was once a safe street for Nikisha and her friends has become a place she cannot leave her children unwatched. Fear of violence and drugs now plagues every decision Nikisha makes for her children's future.

Nikisha sees a community that has changed and is continually changing. What was once a strong community has become disconnected and uncaring. From her window, Nikisha sees the world changing for her neighbors, now in their own struggles with the new limitations of welfare reform. She knows that she is among the fortunate few who have both the support from her family and the work experience to help mitigate her fears. She can see the fear of her neighbors who have been on welfare for all or most of their lives, and those who have been caught in its cycle for generations. It is the vision of these things, and the promise of a new future for her children, that drives Nikisha to continue to fight, to grow, and to learn.

Today, Nikisha feels prepared for her future. She

possesses a quiet strength that seems to come from the knowledge that she can withstand instability, pressure, tragedy, and loss. She feels confident in her skills and in the experience she has gained. Finishing her training at SBEC is a triumph in itself, but in the light of the obstacles that slowed and impeded her progress, the accomplishment is remarkable. She wants a better life, a better home, and a better job. Nikisha believes education is the best path to a future for herself and her children that will be unmarked by desperation and liberated from the chains of poverty. The glorious red and gold winged phoenix of mythology is symbolic of rising to new life. As the bird senses the end of its life drawing near, it builds a nest to be a funeral pyre. The nest is lit on fire by the sun. The phoenix is consumed by the flames only to emerge again from its ashes. Nikisha's life will change forever when she finishes the Welfare-to-work program. She will die to the old welfare system and rise out of its ashes to a new life of financial independence. It is only through the strength of knowing who she is that Nikisha may realize her full potential.

FEEDING THE HUNGRY IS A GREATER WORK THAN RAISING THE DEAD.

Saint John Chrysostom

TROUBLES SURVIVED
by Marie Quinn

October

"I heard," he says.

Betty looks up from pages of notes on a table at the back of the library during the first interview for this story.

"I heard all about it." The man in the dark security uniform turns down the last aisle lined with book shelves. The name on his visor cap is the same as the last employer on the page listing Betty's job losses, which she has catalogued under "Troubles Survived."

Betty, age 52, looks down. The large girth of her stomach expands with hurt. Behind her glasses, tears leak out. She brushes them away before they streak down the round fullness of her cheeks.

"He's a troublemaker," she says, nodding towards the last aisle. She shakes her head and takes a long, labored breath. On the exhale, Betty shuffles the papers in her hand back to page two where she wanted blank space reserved.

Betty's brain boots up again like a library computer programmed to direct what goes where in pages of categories, lists, and details. "Now I remember," she smiles. "Add this right here." She taps at the last number in the list entitled "Blessings."

"Number eight: I never hold on to ANY negative

feelings, not any at all, for ANY length of time.... After they fired me, I sent them a 'thank you' letter."

* * *

Welfare reform was the reason Betty accepted the security guard position. "I was one of the people that the welfare reform hit," she stated. "My two-year time was up in March. They pulled me from training at GECAC (Greater Erie Community Action Center), for general office practice at SBEC through SPOC, a welfare-to-work program which can pay for training. They put me in Job Search. If I hadn't accepted the job, I would have been sanctioned." Betty understood that to mean she would be "cut off cash assistance."

As a security guard, Betty had a variety of assignments on first to third shifts at $5.25 an hour. She stated she liked the job, especially noting a courthouse assignment where she checked people through the metal detector at the entrance. After six months of employment, Betty was fired "because I overslept just once. It surprised me, but they said they had reports that I had been dozing."

She further explained, "Oversleeping, people do that sometimes. It wasn't on purpose, but I was sick and I didn't know it at the time." When she accepted the position in March, Betty did know that she had sleep apnea which causes breathing to stop countless times during the night. "I had been sleeping with oxygen and a C-pap machine set at 16. Six is normal and the maximum you can set it at is 20. But then all of a sudden, I got worse. I really believe that if they hadn't fired me, I would be dead.

I told them 'thank you' for saving my life."

Betty emphasized, "My ordinary sleep time is one to four hours a night of good sound sleep. It's enough. It's wonderful for me. During the sleep problem, I was sleeping eighteen to twenty hours a day. I would fall asleep all the time. People would make fun of it. I tried to shut myself away, but I'm not a sit-at-home person, so I continued going to the doctors."

While in Job Search, just prior to accepting the security position, Betty was offered work in a plastics plant. She got a doctor's verification that she could not stand all day. "I turned the job down because I had gained 50 pounds in two days, and they couldn't figure out why. The doctor arranged for payment for me to go to Weight Watchers®."

Betty's work history prior to welfare reform included many diverse jobs. Starting in February 1995 she worked part-time at $4.80 an hour as a homeless outreach aide for a program whose "grant ran out" in 1997. She helped the homeless by assessing their needs and giving intake appointments so that other staff members could give medical referrals. This was her favorite job because "I'm the best resource person in the city. I know everywhere there is to get help. I remember whole phone numbers after hearing them only once. I'm a walking phone book." According to Betty, her salary went up to $5.15 an hour.

In 1979, Betty earned $7.00 an hour at a factory where she was an inside/outside grinder. She received training for this work through government funding. She lost the job "due to health." Betty stated that she suffered two weeks of intense abdominal pain during which she lost 35 pounds; she was hospitalized for an ovarian cyst. Female health problems persisted. She finally had surgery in 1986. In her initial interview, Betty listed being a "cancer survivor" under "Troubles Survived" and "Blessings" because it gave her "a positive attitude."

Prior to 1979, Betty's many jobs included math teacher at an adult education center, bartender, baker, and preschool teacher's aide. She also worked every position in a department store from setting up shelves to operating the cash register.

In October, despite her work experience, Betty was "really, honestly broke." She explained that because she received one paycheck from the security firm during this month, she was not eligible for cash assistance from welfare. "I've been homeless twice, and I'm headed there again. I can't pay my rent this month, plus I owe $1,000 each for gas and electricity. I paid September's rent with my daughter's SSI (Supplemental Security Income) check, and SSI is saying that because she was placed in a detention home with a residential program that could help her, I shouldn't have picked that check up. It's real scary. But I do not want SSI. That's for people with no initiative who don't have anything goin' in their lives. Sure, some really need it, but not me. I do have physical problems, but I'm going to overcome them."

In the past, being homeless was one of Betty's big

gest troubles. She and her children survived by living with friends on two separate occasions. To prevent history from repeating itself, Betty's plan in October included applying for welfare again, which would not solve her financial problems. "I would get $205 a month and the rent is $325," she said. Betty's strongest hopes for paying her debts were prayer and an optimistic attitude which she believes really solves a lot of problems.

November

Late Saturday morning, parents and grandparents parade with wide-eyed children up and down the sunny side of the dock. Only a few cross over to the shady side where a line of people have been fishing for hours. Betty and her grandson set down their fishing gear near a man and his two sons who wait quietly for still more crappies to nip at the bait.

"Look out!" Betty's big frame jumps as she shouts and points at a running child about fifty feet away. The man and his boys turn to watch both parents snatch up their toddler near the water's edge.

"Some people just don't know how to take care of kids!" Betty exclaims. The father-son fishing team returns its gaze to the steel blue water.

"Gimme fifty cents." Her twelve-year-old grandson tugs at Betty's black windbreaker.

"What'd I tell you at McDonald's, Joshua?" Betty asks, still excited. She tones down to a whisper: "I don't have much money."

"But they're catchin' crappies with minnows," Joshua nods at the silent trio.

Betty places two quarters in her grandson's hand. He steps into a victory dance with the brisk morning wind. Layers of brand name sportswear flatten against his lean body as he stirs up a flock of seagulls.

"Leave them dirty birds alone!" Betty shouts. Her frown softens into a smile as she watches his Tommy Hilfiger® hat bob closer to the bait shop. "Joshua's a wonderful kid. I did a good job," she insists.

Betty looks down at the worms she paid a buck fifty for a half hour ago and adds with a long yawn, "So all we catch is slimy gobies instead of sweet-tastin' crappies." She shakes the need for sleep from her head, looks out at the bay through black sunglasses and pronounces, "It's okay. Look at this. Isn't it beautiful? Look how relaxing it is."

Ten minutes later, while fussing with a minnow he wants to hook just right, Joshua makes his grandmother smile again. "You do it," he convinces her, "'cause you're the best fisherwoman."

* * *

Betty learned to fish in 1975 because she wanted her four children, and the grandchild she raised from infancy to age ten, to be well-rounded. They were all busy with activities every night of the week. She emphasized that she alone navigated a schedule that included football, soccer, scouts, karate, baseball, modeling, basketball and babysitting classes. Betty also arranged for her two youngest to join a walking tour of black history "down south." Her son took seven years of ballet and jazz, because "it keeps you in shape...and teaches you to listen, to obey."

For the most part, Betty was a single mom. "I seem to hook up with the wrong men as partners in life," she admits. "The men I had relationships with, they all had other girlfriends and I wasn't real good dealing with that." According to Betty, when the father of the two oldest whom she lived with for ten years "got good jobs it was 'bye-bye, Betty.' They finally caught up with him when my daughter was sixteen, so he paid support for about a year." Betty claimed that the second father paid just $12.50 a week in support for each of his two children, despite having a good factory job. "He owns all kinds of rental property. He owns cars, trucks, boats, motorcycles," she added.

Betty explained why both men were even more negligent with emotional support for their children: "There's no way to support your child except to get on welfare, and when you get on welfare you have to go file for support. You don't have a choice about it. And they, the fathers, always get mad about that; so the way to punish you is to hurt your kids."

According to Betty, her own dad was an alcoholic who fathered twelve children. Betty's mother "worked her whole life. I was her main problem child. I was the oldest and the first to do everything; but she loved me. She didn't believe in you havin' a baby without marriage."

As a teenager, Betty got pregnant. Her first baby was given up for adoption. Her last baby was stillborn. Because of the financial burden of raising the other four, plus her grandchild, she had not been able to afford a cemetery stone for the baby. "I was brought up in the church. God made me able to deal with a lot," she said.

Betty also raised her own children "in the church." After coping with their teenage rebellions, she doubted her parenting ability. "I didn't do the best job people thought I could do," she said. However, since her two oldest married and settled down, she felt her methods weren't wrong. Because her grandchild could benefit from his mother's positive family life with new brothers and sisters, she said, "I decided it wasn't fair to be selfish and hang on to him. I let his mom have custody of him. He comes to visit. I try to send money, and they let him come up."

In November, Betty's 16-year-old daughter continued to come home for visits. "She was better." Betty affirmed. She explained that this was why she used her daughter's check for rent: "I appealed the thing because I used it for what I was supposed to. I thought she was coming home, and if I hadn't paid the rent, I wouldn't have had a home for her to come to."

Betty summarized her November financial situation: "I had no money—period!" She received no financial help from her 18-year-old son who was living with her. "When he had a job and he was stayin' with me, just him, he paid his way," Betty explained. His girlfriend and her child were also residing in the apartment. Betty stated, "She figured she didn't owe any money, and she was the only one with an income. They buy their own food, but don't help with the bills." Betty commented with downcast eyes, "I can't kick him out. If I did that, I'd never see him. We wouldn't have any kind of relationship."

December

At 11:50 a.m. on December 21, just inside the City Mission, a woman in a man's wool coat takes number 302 and shuffles two shy preschoolers through the double doors.

Beyond a sea of knit caps and Santa hats, coffee, juice and sandwiches, Betty shouts above a Christmas carol, "I can help you over here."

The woman proceeds to the second of three stations set up to serve the 450 families assigned to come in from 10:00 a.m. until 1:00 p.m. for free Christmas dinner fixings.

Beneath a wreath decorated with an angel that has no face, Betty sits at a card table which holds two stacks of paper, each 75 pages thick. They hold the eligible names and addresses she must cross off before passing people through.

Betty's hair is perfectly curled. Her cartoon bird tee shirt is perfectly crisp. Her smile is patient as she watches the woman weave her children through the curved aisle.

"I haf...the ID," the woman offers in broken English.

"It's Betty. One second." Betty takes off her glasses to squint at the names in tiny print midway down a page.

"Darn glasses," she sighs and writes "large" on the ticket. "There you go. Take this and follow the aisle through that door."

While she finishes the directions, Betty focuses on confusion at the next table. "No, listen," she interrupts, "He's listed here." She points and shuffles paper. "Wait a minute. I'm missing the 'B' page."

She looks up to the right and calls to the woman now hesitating near the next table. "No. Keep goin'. See the door over there. Yeah, that one.... What happened to my 'B' page?"

In the next hour, the 'B' page is forgotten as all three stations serve a steady stream of people. Betty's voice often roars above the rush, then muffles to a whisper as she relates personal problems during lulls in the line:

"She was already seen. I took care of her at this table."

"I go to the clinic out of town on December 30," Betty confides.

"They think something's wrong with my ovaries."

"You wanna sit down there? Nobody's free yet, but get your ID out."

"I was tired," Betty mumbles, "so I let this guy move my car for me. He backed it into the soup kitchen's car. Now I've got to report it."

"Hey, kids. Stop kickin' the chairs."

"It's lonely in the apartment," Betty sighs. "The landlord made my son and his family move out."

"Sure, I'll be here tomorrow and December 23, eight to four-thirty."

* * *

Over the past twenty-five years, according to Betty, she has been a committed volunteer despite financial woes, health problems, or family crises. At the City Mission, she has normally worked two to three days a week and on most holidays. However, she admitted, "They let me sleep for two hours during food packing yesterday."

In addition, Betty stated that she volunteers at the soup kitchen where she helps cook and serve food once a week. Once a month, while the program operated, she drove to a church where she packed more bags and boxes of give-away groceries. She has also helped with Special Olympics and at a homeless shelter.

Many volunteer efforts centered around her children and grandchild. "We couldn't pay for the programs. There were scholarships where I had to volunteer," she commented. She also served as a cub scout assistant, brownie leader and at a grade school finger printing campaign.

Betty was instrumental in many parents' associations when her children were in school. She had been an active member of various committees from strategic planning for the school district to finance, personnel and the policy council for Headstart. She served in a wide range of key positions including chairperson, treasurer, parliamentarian, state and national representative, as well as a Headstart aide.

Betty also was the neighborhood babysitter. "I kept everybody's kids because I had to be there for mine. I took 15 to 20 kids trick or treating, got 'em into different sport activities, took 'em to parks. If welfare reform had happened when the kids were little," Betty surmised, "I don't know if it would have worked for me. I really needed to raise my own kids. I mean, I wasn't being lazy. I was busy doing something valuable and constructive. I collected kids because there was nobody there for them except me."

Now that her children are older, she collects grandchildren and step-grandchildren for summer visits. "Just as many as can go to vacation bible school. They stay like a week to two weeks. I think everybody needs God in their life," she affirmed.

According to Betty, as she raised her children, she spent probably at least a hundred hours a week on volunteer efforts. "And the kids went with me to just about everything. I didn't really do babysitters," she said, "'cause I always taught my kids to trust friends and family the least. You need to watch out for strangers, but friends and family are the ones who can get you. You know, I tend not to trust people; I'm sorry about that, but friends and family have hurt me. And they have easy access to you because they're familiar people."

"I probably volunteered double what most people work," Betty reiterated. "I couldn't afford to fund my kids financially. Volunteering was a way of paying back so I'm not takin' something for nothing. Plus it kept my mind off my troubles."

In December, Betty's mind was troubled with possibly moving to a shelter. She was grateful that, for her, the landlord reflected the spirit of the season. Although her son and his family had to leave "because they weren't paying any money," he allowed Betty to stay as long as she checked in daily with him. "We discussed everything I did as far as trying to get him paid.... I'm lucky he stuck by me because I'm not a person who could ever stay in a shelter. You know, I have a very strong personality."

A New Year—A New Millennium

On the third Sunday in January, a gray, 1988 Chevy Beretta creeps into the church parking lot beside cars now dusted with snow. Betty emerges from the driver's seat and shuffles past the badly damaged front end of her car. Inside the tiny white country church, she stops to catch her breath before joining the Coffee and Donut Club downstairs.

Just as the tenth and last person begins to list blessings God gave her in the past week, Betty opens the door and murmurs, "Sorry I'm late." She gulps in air and exhales, "I overslept."

The minister, his wife and two others smile, rise and move in closer. Another chair is added at the big wooden table. Once the group resettles, Betty's labored breathing continues as the speaker concludes her brief sharing.

"Well, I'm worse," Betty says breathlessly "but better. God's been so good to me this week. Wednesday I got a new machine to help my sleep apnea. It's a bipap, with five

54

liters of oxygen for sounder sleep. I slept so good. I only snored once. I may not sleep during the sermon today!"

Her listeners nod and laugh. Betty tries to catch her breath and adds in a compromised voice, "My hands and feet are numb, and I've got these cold-like symptoms, and I'm out of breath quicker. But this time I'm gonna work with the doctors so they can take care of side effects."

Betty quickly continues, "And I found out it was Betty to use my daughter's check to help pay the rent, and I got an OK to get SSI checks, too. Just for now. I'm on it for six months while they decide. I just applied last month. Some people wonder how I got on so fast. All I can say is the only thing that gets me by is complete faith in God. And then on Friday...." Betty's chest heaves in a deep breath. The group leader sneaks in a signal to "wrap it up."

"Well, on Friday," Betty continues, "I found out I got accepted for the citizens' police academy classes. So I've just been sayin' 'Thank you, God... Thank you, God' all week long."

Betty's abundant sharing results in louder breathing through bible discussion and dismissal for the worship celebration upstairs. "Somethin's got to be done about this breathing," Betty confides to the woman next to her on the stairs. "When I was out line dancin', I could hardly do the electric slide."

When the service begins, Betty nods and listens with wide-eyed attention as the minister reads, "Let everything that has breath praise the Lord!"

Although her voice is barely audible as she sings three hymns, Betty remains awake. When the long sermon ends and she has not dozed off even once, she sings with a smile: "When I fall down, You pick me up. When I am dry, You fill my cup. You are my all in all."

After worship, Betty lingers to talk to another parishioner: "I don't know if I can keep drivin' out here. I'm prayin' but I might lose my license. I hit a fire truck. I could have fought to keep my eyes open, but I closed them. My car's a wreck, and I've got to pay a $101.00 fine."

Before her listener can comment, a young girl bounces between them waving a cookie order sheet. "Ooh!" Betty exclaims as she checks off an order for five boxes. "On February 1, I'll have my SSI check. I can pay for these!"

* * *

From February 1 through her final interview for this story on April 5, Betty paid far more important bills than her cookie order. "Now I'm actually, officially on SSI," she said. Her SSI check, according to Betty, was more than double the amount of welfare cash assistance. While it did not allow her to pay debts down to zero, she stated she was making progress.

Having a steady income to rely on for rent payment was in direct contrast to her end-of-the-year financial status. Betty discussed how welfare checks arrived sporadically. "When I finally did get $102.50, I gave the landlord twenty dollars of that check, and they cut me off welfare again. I guess the man didn't do his paper-work right. I had made copies. When they saw the copies, they reinstated me, so for January 14, I got another check. Out of that check, I paid forty dollars rent. There's no way you can promise to pay somebody when you don't know what's gonna happen next."

"I owe a gigantic amount on rent still, but I gave him [the landlord] a thousand dollar bill," Betty stated. When questioned about the one-bill payment, Betty countered, "Well, no, I gave him ten one-hundred dollar bills." When asked if SSI was the reason she was able to make that payment, Betty replied, "Basically, it's due to having an income finally, you know."

Her teenaged daughter, who was now living at home, received SSI benefits. Betty explained, "They haven't officially taken my daughter off. She should be off any day if this caseworker gets his stuff together. And I've got one of her checks, but I'm not gonna take any more."

Because she now had an income, according to Betty, she received help with utility bills. "Every time I make a $26 electric bill payment, they'll make a hundred and some dollar payment towards that bill, as long as I pay on time. If I don't, I'm out of the program," she said. Betty also stated that there was help with her gas bill. However, she added, "the phone one I had to do myself."

Betty was most pleased that after 14 years she could finally pay for a cemetery stone for her stillborn child's grave. She cried while describing how it showed Jesus and "an angel or baby or somethin'" reaching out to one another. She felt that the $175 price was "a favor." It was a scratched stone.

Betty was excited that she could contribute more to her church. "I tithe better now than I ever did in my life. I let God take control, and He does a lot of things that I didn't dare do. He gives me things and He tells me to give them back, and I'll be richer for it, and it's been the truth."

Betty also discussed the bills relating to three auto accidents which happened in December. She had to appear in court due to the accident with the fire truck, and has been "paying on" the fine. In addition, the day after the accident with the soup kitchen vehicle, she hit another car. "It was that slushy snow and either I slid into this lady's mirror or she was over too far." She noted, "Her mirror got knocked off. But I'm to blame for all of these. That's the bottom line. Luckily, I had been paying full coverage all these years on my car."

Her insurance coverage enabled her to replace the car damaged in the fire truck accident. After this accident, Betty was still able to drive her car, but not for long. "My daughter and I were driving out to church," she related, "and all of a sudden the hood went—whap—against the windshield when I was driving 65 miles per hour. We got the car stopped but the hood was all crumpled."

Car troubles persisted when the motor in the replaced vehicle blew up three weeks later on the trip back from the clinic where she was told she might have ovarian cancer. Although this car, a '91 Buick Skylark, was purchased as is, according to Betty, the dealer replaced it with a '90 Buick Century. "I had to pay about $500 more. I'll sign the second insurance check over to him. It seems to be oBetty," she shrugged.

Betty believed that her health was also Betty, although she said that two blood tests for ovarian cancer were bad. "The doctors at the clinic say they don't think that I have cancer. They said they told the doctor here that I need to see a specialist, that I might have a bladder or urinary problem; but he hasn't sent me to a doctor yet 'cause he's a quack. I may end up going on my own. I don't know who to pick," Betty explained.

After receiving the news that she may have the same disease which took her mother's life, Betty missed two appointments for this final interview. However, she was early for the third and affirmed, "It's not a scare for me because I have a personal relationship with God. If He decides it's my time to die then it's my time to die. I could sit back and wait to die or stay busy doing things to be a productive, useful human being."

"I'm back in Weight Watchers and I'm riding a bike at the YMCA. I'm going to get better," Betty promised. "I want to work. I don't want to just volunteer. I really want to be an airline reservation agent. There's a great job out there that's meant just for me."

THE WELL FED PERSON AND THE HUNGRY ONE DO NOT SEE THE SAME THING WHEN THEY LOOK UPON A LOAF OF BREAD.

Rumi

FARING WELL OFF WELFARE
by Mary Amthor

Nicole's voice is very sweet. Her words bubble like water in a mountain stream; her thoughts meander and sparkle. Streams all lead somewhere, and it is clear that Nicole is going places, too. Her gentleness belies a steely core which, she says, was won from the school of hard knocks.

Nicole's dance with public assistance began about the same time as welfare reform. In 1995, after an unsuccessful marriage, Nicole became the single parent of two little boys. Short stays with her mother, and then with her father and stepmother, helped at the beginning, but soon the 22-year-old was truly on her own.

A high school diploma doesn't provide much financial defense against a world demanding bigger and better educational tools, and Nicole was soon in the dole lines. She had never thought she would be in this situation.

"There's no quality of life when you're on welfare," says Nicole. "You feel like a beggar. You have no money for anything else but your basic needs. You can't get out of your house; you can't get out of your yard."

Nicole received $416 a month for rent only and about $300 per month in food stamps. But with utility costs added to rents that averaged $350-400 each month, there was nothing left over.

"People don't realize that when you're on welfare, taking the kids out to get ice cream is a big deal. That's something that most folks do without thinking about it. Pack the kids up in the nice, new car and go out to get something to eat. Well, if you're on welfare, you can't do that!"

Picture this: a small, gray house neatly nestled upon a hillside in western Pennsylvania. A multi-textured, colorful English garden wraps itself around the front of the home. The tiny two-bedroom cottage is well appointed and everything is in its place. Papers are organized carefully around the home computer. There is not a dish to be seen in the kitchen sink which is framed by carefully scrubbed countertops. Timmy, five-years old, is singing along with a Disney video. Two country cats are curled by the front door and a full pot of freshly brewed coffee fills the residence with an inviting scent. Nicole fixes a steady gaze on me as she speaks. A wavy, blond bob frames her deep blue eyes and easy smile. Strong, muscular hands grip a coffee mug. A blue sweatshirt and jeans mask Nicole's newly won slim figure. She talks about having vowed to get fit and lose weight upon re-entering single life—one goal accomplished. Ambition and hope fill Nicole's eyes as she talks about her pending career in social work, a fulfilling relationship with her boyfriend, and a life that feels fairly under control. This woman is like a weeble doll: she may wobble, but she doesn't fall down.

* * *

The Personal Responsibility and Work Opportunity

Reconciliation Act of 1996 (PRWORA) requires participation in work-related activities, as defined by each state, within 24 months of receiving assistance.

Nicole wasn't bothered by the new welfare-to-work regulations. She longed for a good job, but knew that was impossible without training. And she didn't always have time for work and training.

Studies have shown that skills acquired during one semester of post-secondary education can, for some, improve annual income by up to $10,000. All states require people to work while on welfare, but several states allow course work to count for that requirement. In other words, you need skills and education to make money, and you need money to permanently wean yourself from welfare.

Nicole turned to Saint Benedict Education Center (SBEC) for help. She was surprised that they required self-esteem programs before job training.

"They offered wacky, off the wall things that you'd never think would help you feel better. For example, a woman came to talk about flatulence! She taught us that everyone has embarrassing moments." Nicole laughs as she explains that the job market can be a frightening place for women who are not comfortable with themselves. The mere thought of dealing with menstrual cycles or flatulence can be enough to send them running. These kinds of courses help women to conquer almost any hurdles that the job world offers. "The self-esteem programs almost liberated me. They made me realize that

I'm a human being and I have the same emotions as President Clinton or Julia Roberts!"

From January to August of 1997, Nicole took part in a program sponsored by the Job Training Partnership of Pennsylvania (JTPA), SBEC's Single Point of Contact (SPOC), and the Office of Children and Youth. She enrolled in SBEC's Personal Care Technician courses and two weeks after graduating found a job at Lakeshore Community Services.

The job turned out to be a double-edged sword. Two weeks after she started, Nicole lost her childcare payments. She had to pay a sizeable fee for her children's childcare, not an easy task while earning $8.63 an hour. Welfare would pay for her children's health insurance; fortunately, her employer provided insurance for her after a probationary period. Nicole just thanks God she is healthy.

Then, things got really tough. Nicole's brother was killed by a drunk driver, and her other brother Mark, 16, moved in with her. When Lakeshore Community Services put Nicole on 3rd shift she thought Mark's presence was a godsend. He could watch the boys. But instead, Nicole's home became the headquarters for teenage parties, and in early 1998 they were all evicted. This led to two more moves. "Every time I worked, it was a teeter-totter. I never knew what was happening at home. I had to put up with Mark having friends over so I could keep working."

So, how did Nicole end up in her idyllic home? The Johnsons.

"They have been the turning point of my life. They have given me moral support and family support. The Johnson's love my kids, they call them their grandchildren."

Betty and Bill Johnson are now renting the small house with the big garden on their property to Nicole and her boys. Their close proximity is a big comfort to Nicole.

Nicole took a huge step toward her goals after finishing the 1999-2000 school year at Gannon University with high grades—all while working up to 40 hours a week at Lakeshore Community Services. She intends to complete a four-year major in criminal justice and social work.

"I want to be in a job that makes me happy, where I can help people, where I can change people's lives, like Betsy does."

Betsy Weiss is a case manager at Saint Ben's who has helped many people remove themselves from welfare's grip. Although she agrees that the new welfare-to-work laws are getting folks off the dole, she warns that the new life they walk into is not necessarily better. Often it is better, according to Betsy, but one of the major difficulties is that welfare subsidies decrease in relation to the amount of money earned, she says.

Even though Nicole had always intended to work, she feels her experience could have been far less painful and stressful if her university credits had counted as work and if she didn't have a two-year time limit hanging over her head.

"I think it's unhealthy for a woman to have time

limits set for her when she's a mother. All her children should be over five years of age when they're taken off of welfare. Everything that happens to a mother happens to her children. The feelings of guilt are intense—it's the strongest bond," she says, giving Timmy a cuddle, "between a mother and her child. Is someone taking care of my child? Is someone loving them?"

"Clearly, working has had an impact on my grades. I'm not complaining," says Nicole bravely, "I know I can handle anything. But I would like to see women in congregate living arrangements while they're at school: not paying rent, not working; children staying at home with a daycare worker coming in so that no mother has to snatch her child out of bed at 4:30 a.m. and expose her to the cold and rain. I would like to see the state buy homes throughout the community, just for women. Women need a social safety net that not only includes funds, but emotional help, physical help and someone to talk to—other mothers who are struggling like they are." She points out this might not be for everyone, but it should be an option.

This, too, could help prevent the "bad boyfriend" scenario. Nicole admits to having a bad boyfriend during her lowest time, something she let happen because she was feeling so down and bad about herself. During this time, her youngest son, Timmy, was expelled from day care, diagnosed with attention deficit, hyperactive disorder, and had to be bused a half hour each morning and afternoon into a special facility. Nicole thinks the relationship with her boyfriend at this time was partly responsible for Timmy's problems.

"This really threw a bone in the works," Nicole laments, clearly sharing the pain and frustration that her child was experiencing.

The difference between a mom in cheap student housing and a student in cheap student housing is clear: a mother's key concern is providing the most secure, stable and loving environment possible for her child or children. Earning $200 a week before taxes doesn't make that possible. That's why Nicole thought congregate living should be an option for all single mothers (and single fathers) choosing to pursue higher education while on welfare. This arrangement would make a degree and ultimately a permanent divorce from welfare possible.

Over the last five years, Nicole, now 27, has been through a separation, divorce, single parenthood, the dole lines, poor self-image, a bad boyfriend, unreliable baby-sitters, several housing problems and moves. But her pile of laurels is growing: two healthy, happy boys, now 5 and 7, a healthy romantic relationship, a close friendship with her brother, a solid home environment for her children, self-esteem classes, job training, a promotion and raise at Lakeshore Community Services, and the successful completion of year one in a four-year degree program.

Before Nicole darts out to pick up seven-year-old Billy from the bus stop, she sums up her philosophy, "I know from life experience not to bet everything on one option. I get by, but I have no money saved. I'm kind of open to where I will go. I believe God has been a driving force."

I think Nicole can be sure that God won't leave her—that she will continue receiving God's guidance.

[1] Associated Press. "Critics argue state welfare rule does more harm than good." *Erie Morning News*. Tuesday, May 30, 2000. P. 1a, 7a. Vol. 44, No. 103.

THE FEEDING OF THOSE WHO ARE HUNGRY IS A FORM OF CONTEMPLATION.

Simone Weil

DWELLING IN POSSIBILITY
by Mary Hembrow Snyder

Dear Shonda,

I began this "assignment" as an essay and by the time I got to the end of the first page I realized I just wanted to write you a letter. Letter writing is a threatened form of communication today for all kinds of reasons, not the least of which is that it takes *time*—time most of us no longer feel we have—time to be reflective, time to say something from the heart, time to honor a relationship worth nurturing, time to dare to be personal in an increasingly impersonal world. And even though I am guilty myself of believing writing a letter takes too much time, I owe this to you, Shonda. *You* took time for me, to let me, a total stranger, peek a bit into your precious life. Out of respect for you and what you have become, I want, now, to take time for you, to write you a story about yourself, which, one day at a time, will continue to remind you of how far you have come on your journey to freedom and wholeness.

During an interview she gave in the early 1980s, the poet, essayist, and cultural critic, Audre Lorde, remarked, "...the only kind of pain that is intolerable is pain that is wasteful, pain from which we do not learn. And I think we must learn to distinguish between the two." If there is anyone who understands the truth of

Lorde's insight, it is you Shonda!

Formerly, you were a woman caught in the moribund cycle of welfare and/or underemployment by dint of circumstances and poor choices; today, Shonda, you are a graduate of Saint Benedict Education Center where you earned a certificate as a Human Services Associate which enabled you to become fully employed. Formerly, you were a woman obsessed with and dominated by your craving for drugs and alcohol; today, Shonda, you are clean and sober and have been so for three years now. Formerly, you were a woman who dropped out of high school at the age of 17 because you were bored and restless; today, Shonda, you are eagerly pursuing your GED. Formerly, you were a woman blind to your own potential and wrestling with the agony of low self- esteem, today, Shonda, you jubilantly exclaim, "Not only am I an inspiration to my grandchildren, *I am an inspiration to myself*!"

Indeed, Shonda, you are an inspiration to all of us who have the privilege of knowing you. Your painful journey over the years, as you struggled to reinvent yourself and recreate your life has not been wasted. No. On the contrary, you have learned a great deal from your pain every single day of your difficult and rewarding life. Most significantly, you have learned the fundamental lesson every African-American woman must learn in this racist, sexist society of ours or perish tragically, namely, you, Shonda, "dwell in possibility," and nobody but you can abort that truth!

Nonetheless, you did not learn this lesson easily. There were years, by your own admission, when you refused to learn anything! It took suffering, failure, discouragement, despair and prison; it took inner strength, determination, a fragile but tenacious hope, and a recently discovered well of self-confidence; most of all it took people who cared about you—your mother, your daughter Samantha, your fiancé Mike, your grand-children, your son Bob, your youngest child Laura, Sister Miriam, Sister Audrey, Patty Lawson, and a host of others—to help you see you were capable of living a different and better kind of life.

Remember when your first child, Robert, was born in 1973? You were only a junior in high school. Often you got in trouble, as you said, "because of my mouth," and often you were suspended. You despised school then. You told me, "I wanted to be grown." You also felt your teachers in high school had little to offer you. Now you know that was probably not true.

In 1975 your second child, Samantha, was born. Being on welfare enabled you to provide for your two children, but you were searching for direction in life, for a sense of who you were. Unfortunately, you found it on the streets, specifically in "The Hood"—that area of east side Erie where drugs, prostitution, bootlegging, gambling, poverty and violence persist like weeds in a neglected garden. This is where you learned to smoke, drink, and use drugs. Such was your way of life until the end of 1991 when you discovered you were pregnant with your third child.

Despite your precarious existence, you wanted this baby to be healthy. Consequently, you quit smoking, stopped using drugs, and gave up alcohol. Your baby was born March 31, 1992 and you named her Laura. Here was potential for conversion, so to speak, for you to turn your life completely around and go consciously in a different and healthier direction. Unfortunately, the temptation to numb the uncertainty, anxiety, and fear which accompanied this potential triumphed. Five months after Laura was born you began using again. Your drug habit consumed you. Where and how you were going to get your next high became your obsession. Crack cocaine became your drug of choice and you began to sell drugs to maintain it.

Eventually you lost your apartment because you chose to feed your addiction rather than pay the rent. You moved to West 18th street—close to "Little Italy"—but regularly visited "The Hood" because that is where you had access to drugs. In time you began to trust "the brothers" who ruled there and you allowed them to turn your home into a market for drug trafficking. In exchange, these men paid your rent, your utilities and gave you and Laura anything you needed. Most of the time, though, Laura lived upstairs with Samantha. In your own way you knew you had to protect this baby from the nefarious environment which held all three of you captive.

On November 1, 1995, however, your life changed once again, painfully so. You were arrested for selling drugs. As you explained it, there was no preliminary hearing even though it was your first offense. The court sentenced you to six to twelve months of probation and put a monitor on you for thirty days. But at least you didn't get sent to jail— at least not this time.

In recounting these events you stated that you had two very nasty parole officers who made your life on probation very difficult. Yet you admitted you continued to use, so when they gave you a random urinalysis it came back positive. This time you were sentenced to six to 12 months in the Erie County Prison even though you asked to go to rehab. Anxious about Laura and how she would be cared for, you signed your maternal rights over to Samantha who was 21 years old at the time. Samantha was the primary person who made the pain of this tragic situation bearable because of the love and compassion she had for you and her little sister.

For a year, you were in and out of prison. While you stopped using drugs, you violated your probation by refusing to stop drinking and this landed you back in jail. You told me this prison experience was unspeakably difficult because they placed you in solitary confinement for three weeks because they insisted that your random urinalysis once again came back positive. You disputed their findings but were powerless to change the situation. By the time your were released in late October the only concern you continued to have was where you were going to get your next drink.

A moment of unrepeatable opportunity came in

1997 when you appeared in front of Judge DiSantis. After talking with you he told you, your probation officer and your counselor from GECAC that if in thirty days they did not find you a bed in a rehabilitation program you were simply to be released. You spent 29 of those 30 days in jail but they did find you a chance for recovery. In March, you willingly went to Colonial House in York, Pennsylvania for 31 days. When you described that experience you said, "I came home in April and have not looked back since."

By mid-1998 you had finished your parole and went back on welfare. You lived with Samantha and Laura and worked several part-time jobs. Increasingly, however, you felt discouraged. Your life seemed to be going nowhere. You and your caseworker, Patty Lawson, discussed possible options. Attending Saint Benedict Education Center was one of them. It turned out, providentially, to be a graced choice. With its holistic approach to job training and job placement, surrounded by its caring and supportive teachers and staff, you flourished. How often you commented that if it were not for Sister Miriam, Sister Audrey and Patty, you would not have made it through the program. They encouraged you, challenged you, and believed in you—key ingredients for your ongoing growth and success.

Other persons who upheld and supported you in your efforts to reconstruct your life included your mother, Rita Annie, your incredibly faithful daughter Samantha, and your devoted fiancé Mike. Of him you tell an endearing story. You recalled for me that one day you came home and remarked to Mike, "I feel like getting high today." He responded by kissing you and said, "There! Are you high enough?" Mike has been faithfully present to you and in his own no-nonsense but loving way, he continues to remind you that you always have a choice: you can be married to him or to the streets.

Wisely you continue to choose Mike, to choose sobriety, to choose to stay clean, to choose LIFE. You have realized that you no longer need drugs in your life—that they have only caused you, in truth, misery. Because of this realization and your daily fidelity to your true self, to your hard-won success at St. Ben's, to your family and your future, you have been able to dream new dreams.

Modest though they are, they give renewed hope and meaning to everything you undertake. You dream of maintaining a decent paying job, of getting your GED, of obtaining your driver's license. You are aware of your own potential for growth like never before. You have discovered the courage and inner strength you need to be true to yourself no matter how persistent the temptations to do otherwise. Because of this you see life with new eyes. Now you recognize more clearly the love your grandchildren have for you and the deep bond you share with your daughter Samantha who has always, *always,* been there for you, no matter the circumstances.

Today you have your own apartment, your family, and your impending marriage to Mike. Today you have hope in your heart and your future is bright with expectation.

Clearly, in the words of the poet Emily Dickinson, you, Shonda, "dwell in possibility." Why? Because you did not waste your pain; rather, you allowed it to teach you what you had to learn to become all you are capable of becoming. No wonder each day you awaken you can look in the mirror and say with abundant joy, "*I am an inspiration to myself!*"

And to us Shonda. And to us.

Congratulations! Know, wherever life takes you, that this is my heartfelt prayer for you:

> *May the One who created you in wholeness meet your*
> *needs when you call!*
> *May the Name of Love be your protection and rise up*
> *in your heart as a tower of strength!*
> *May all you have given in gratitude and with open*
> *hands be returned to you a hundredfold!*
> *May your heart's desires and all your plans be fulfilled*
> *in due season!*   Psalm 20
>
> (from *Psalms for Praying* by Nan C. Merrill)

Respectfully yours,
Mary Hembrow Snyder

POVERTY
IS A PAIN
BUT NOT
A DISGRACE.

Scottish

LUCY'S SUCCESS STORY
by Mukami Ireri

There is one thing that Lucy adamantly refuses to share with the reading public, even when assured of anonymity: the circumstances surrounding her birth almost 30 years ago in Erie, Pennsylvania. "Erie is a small community and people will figure out it's me, even if you don't use my name," she explains. "I just don't want that part of my life out on the street."

That stubbornness is typical of Lucy, a tall black woman with a mega-watt smile who, in just seven years, has transformed herself from a welfare mom living in the projects into the administrator of a nurse aide training program for a globally-known non-profit organization. Recently, Lucy was approved for a Habitat For Humanity house and hopes to move her seven-year-old son and six-month-old daughter into their brand new three-bedroom home in about a year.

But things have not always looked this hopeful for Lucy. Born on July 18, 1970, she recalls a childhood fraught with hopelessness, confusion and pain, although her very early years, according to her mother, seemed quite promising. "She was very talkative in kindergarten," remembers her mother, Nancy, cradling Lucy's newborn daughter in her arms. "Just a sweet, lovable kid. The change in her didn't start until she was in fifth grade." The "change" was, for the most part, withdrawal. The friendly, outgoing kid seemed to suddenly retreat into herself, confounding her mother and teachers. "All of a sudden I was getting calls from her teachers saying Lucy wasn't turning in her homework," Nancy recalled. "And on top of that, the teachers said she had become mouthy with them. At first I didn't believe the teachers at all. I thought they were just picking on her."

What Nancy did not know at the time was that a closely-guarded family secret regarding Lucy's birth had been callously and maliciously told to Lucy, leaving her angry, betrayed and distrustful of everyone around her. So her grades continued a downward spiral. Lucy would dutifully do her homework after school knowing full well that she would not turn it in. "I remember going with Lucy to her school's open house around that time and listening to her teachers tell me that she never did her homework," says Nancy. "Yet I had *seen* her do her homework. None of it made sense until I opened her locker and saw a semester's worth of homework stuffed inside."

Soon after that incident mother and daughter had a heart-felt talk about Lucy's beginnings. Her mother sought to reassure Lucy of her love. But Lucy, while acknowledging the love of this remarkable woman, remained angry and deeply distrustful. By the time she entered East High School, Lucy considered herself a lost cause. "I refused to let anyone help me," she says, adding that both the school's principal and English teacher tried very hard to reach out to her. "Whenever they tried to get close to me I'd get very snappy with them." Her social life at school fared no better: "I did not belong to any clique," Lucy observes now, half-amused. "I was too evil to be in a clique. I was in a clique all by myself."

After her high school graduation, Lucy was eager to get out of Erie. "I just wanted to get away from home," she says. Her mother, meanwhile, kept encouraging her to further her education. "I kept telling her that she needed to make plans about her life, beginning with her education," Nancy explains. "But to Lucy I was just a nagging mother."

To satisfy Nancy *and* to get out of Erie, Lucy applied for admission to ICM School of Pittsburgh, a technical and business institute. She was accepted, along with a female cousin who also wanted to leave town. Armed with financial aid, the two young cousins painted Pittsburgh red, attending parties and nightspots until the early hours of the morning. "I wasn't serious about learning anything there and neither was my cousin," Lucy admits. "All we wanted was to get away from home."

But soon that party was over. "After seven months, they cut off our financial aid and we had to come back to Erie." Nancy, disappointed by her daughter's lack of direction, didn't know what else to do. Says Lucy, "She continued nagging and nagging me to get an education; to have a plan. But I didn't want to hear her advice." Instead, Lucy connected with what she openly refers to as "street girls," disappearing from her home in the Franklin Terrace projects for days, and eventually months at a time. She and her new friends never knew from day to day where they would spend the night. "I would go looking for her and sometimes I'd find her in town," recalls Nancy. "And when I did find her I'd plead with her to come back home and live with me. But she wouldn't have any of it."

When Lucy got pregnant, Nancy was not surprised. Nor was she surprised when Lucy announced that her baby's father wanted nothing to do with her or the baby. "That had been my biggest fear all along, unwanted pregnancy. It was happening to good, decent girls from good homes. I did not want that for my daughter." Nevertheless, Nancy realized that her pregnant daughter now needed her support and she proceeded to give it. After her son, Eric, was born, Lucy settled into an apartment near her mother's at Franklin Terrace. So she, like her mother, was now a single mother on welfare.

The realization that she had become part of a cycle that she had so desperately wanted to break hit Lucy very hard. "After my son was born, I was sitting in my apartment one day and I thought: Here I am, a mom, with no skills, no job, just a welfare check. How am I going to take care of my son? I guess that's what pressured me to get out there. I didn't want to do to Eric what had happened to me."

"Out there" turned out be Saint Benedict Education Center. Lucy vaguely remembers being told about the Center's Single Point of Contact (SPOC) program by her welfare case worker and somewhat reluctantly going there to register. "Although I knew that I needed to do something to help myself, I was undecided about what it would be. At the time, in 1992, Lucy and her baby son were living on her $158 a month welfare cash allowance plus less than $200 a month in food stamps. "I was grateful that they gave me the money, but it was tough," she says. "My rent was $83 a month and then there were the utilities. It wasn't enough for the personal things we needed to live on."

The first thing she did at SPOC was basic training in math and reading. Then she was offered a chance to join a new program at the Center called "Medical Office Specialist." In this program she took classes in computer, communication skills, medical terminology and insurance coding. She says the course took about two years to complete, after which she was awarded a certificate.

Looking back, Lucy says she's surprised she stuck with the program. "Don't forget I was very young—21 or 22—and totally uncut, unpolished," she chuckles. "I wasn't used to being around nuns, and I thought they were way too strict. For instance, we were not allowed to chew gum. And I almost flipped when they said we couldn't wear perfume. It was like, 'They're trying to say we stink!'" She says she dealt with these perceived indignities by developing a major attitude problem. "I gave them nothing but attitude. It was either my way or no way."

And she's equally surprised that they stuck by her. "I owe a lot to Saint Benedict Education Center. I now recommend it to everybody. I had to grow up to appreciate what they had done for me. Now I can understand why some-one who has allergies would not want people around them wearing perfume. They could have forced me out, but they didn't. Instead, they stood firm. They were tough with me when I needed it. I needed structure. But they also helped me move along. They gave me the tools I needed to make progress."

After getting her SPOC certificate, Lucy was told that there was a job opening in her field at a major non-profit organization. The staff urged her to go there and fill out an application. "My mom drove me there because I didn't have a car," says Lucy. "We got lost a few times but finally got there and I filled out an application. Then I handed the application to a woman who asked me if I was good at deal-ing with stress. I told her I've been dealing with stress all my life. We chatted for quite a bit. Then she said she'd call me regarding my job application. I thought, 'Yeah, right.'" That same weekend, the phone rang. It was the woman with the job opening, Susan, offering her the job.

When she took that job five years ago, Lucy became the only African-American in the organization. She was also paid the least. At first, she says, she was so grateful about being able to earn a living that she didn't care about her comparatively low pay. And, besides, she acknowledges, she had a lot to learn about her new job as coordinator of her organization's nurse training program, especially dur-ing her first year there.

"Susan, the program director, was my immediate supervisor and she helped me a lot, especially with my writing skills. She would take her red pen and mark errors," reports a grateful Lucy. The two women became good friends; Susan is her children's godmother. Then, last January, Susan abruptly resigned from her position. The organization's administrative manager asked Lucy to take on Susan's job. When Lucy asked if she'd get a pay raise to go with her added workload, she was told there was not enough money in the budget. Still, she continued to do Susan's work, as well as her own.

"I have been hearing about that budget having no money in it ever since I first asked for a raise four years ago," Lucy fumed to me on the phone one evening last February. "Yet," she continued, "each year one of my colleagues gets a raise. How come there's money in the budget for them but not for me?" The following morning, Lucy handed the administrator a letter she had written saying she would not do Susan's work unless she was paid within the position's salary range. She got the raise. "It's $25,000 a year, plus benefits, and I know that's not a lot to most people," Lucy observed. "But don't forget that five years ago my total income, including food stamps, was, at the very most, $358 a *month*."

These days, Lucy seems to be enjoying herself. She's excited about her new house and very grateful that her mortgage will be interest-free. She and her son and daughter will finally be able to leave the projects. She might even marry her daughter's father, who has been very supportive to her, both during and after her pregnancy. Lucy and her mother have a wonderful relationship now, and her mom takes care of the children when Lucy is at work. Both seem to have visited the past, taken a good look at it, and learned from it.

A STRANGER
AND AFRAID
IN A WORLD
I NEVER MADE.

A.E. Housman

ANNA'S STORY
by Mukami Ireri

Anna sits in the neat living room she shares with four women in Erie's east side and considers the historic presidential drama between Al Gore and George W. Bush playing on TV.

"You know what I think? I think George W. Bush is a wet noodle. I have followed this presidential election more closely than any other, and I have paid attention to the issues. I voted for Al Gore because he has better ideas about issues that affect me personally, like Social Security and prescription drugs. But I'm getting sick of this fighting now. I really think they should scrap this whole election and let Clinton run the country for another four years." That said, Anna smiles mischievously and leans back in her seat. She is now ready to review the assorted facts of her life, a life that makes her happy but which, she acknowledges, has had more than its share of ups and downs.

Anna was born to Polish parents in Erie 58 years ago. Her father worked in a factory and her mother was a homemaker. A younger sister completed the family, which extended to her maternal grandparents and aunt, with whom they shared a house. She remembers her early years fondly: Anna, her sister and parents slept upstairs but took all their meals with her grandparents, who lived downstairs.

When Anna was only seven-years-old, her mother

fell ill and died. Grief-stricken, her grandparents vowed to hold the family together, so Anna, her younger sister and dad continued to live with them. A student at nearby St. Stanislaus school, Anna drew comfort from her maternal aunt, who sought to fill the void left by her sister's death. "My aunt was 21 years older than me but she was more like a sister than an aunt to me. She was very outgoing and friendly," Anna recalls. "But it was a very difficult time and to this day I wonder how my life would have been different had my mom not died when I was so young."

More difficulty and turmoil came into her life when her father remarried. The two young sisters moved out of their grandparents' home to live with their dad and step-mother and her two young children. "Her children were approximately my age and she constantly took their side, favoring them over us," Anna says. Even as she grieved for her mother she felt rejected and ostracized in her new home. Anna was now attending Holy Rosary School and the only bright spots in her life were those moments when she could be with her grandparents and her aunt. Her father worked long hours and Anna and her sister spent little time with him. Still, she continued to live with her father's new family until she started   high school.

"When I started high school at St. Benedict Academy, I decided I had had enough and I moved back in with my grandparents. My little sister stayed with my dad but when she got older she also moved out."

High school was a happier time for Anna. "My aunt

really helped me through those teenage years. She was always understanding and helped me come out of my shell."

After she graduated, Anna worked briefly in an office. In her mind, college was not an option. "In those days, after high school you might work for a while but women were expected to look for a husband and settle down," she said. Her father introduced her to his best friend's brother and he and Anna soon married. She gave birth to her first child, a son who is now 32. A daughter followed, and Anna and her husband bought their own house. "Our mortgage was $79 a month," she laughs, adding, "Try and buy a house for that today!" She says they paid off the house in "seven years, seven months and seven days. I tried playing that number in the lottery but never hit, so I'm not sure it's all that lucky after all."

There was not much luck in her marriage, either, even though it lasted 23 years. "It was a very difficult marriage but I felt I had to stick it out, as divorce was frowned upon by the Catholic Church and by society. The majority of women in those days stayed home until their children were grown, and that's what I did. I stayed home and played cards with other wives. But when my husband got home from work it was pure hell. He was both verbally and physically abusive."

Anna says the verbal abuse was at least, if not more, painful than the slaps, kicks and blows she endured, but that she was at a loss about how to end it. She *did* however, figure out how to stop the physical abuses. "One day he came home and beat the hell out of me and I went straight to the emergency room of the hospital where he worked. I told everybody there how I had sustained my injuries. He never *dared* lay a finger on me after that!"

After a bitter divorce, Anna sank into a deep depression. Her husband kept their house. On her own for the first time in her life, Anna moved into an apartment with her son, who was then 20, and teenage daughter. She found a job in a factory and struggled to make ends meet. Both her grandparents were now dead and her aunt—the only other person who had always been there for her in times of emotional and mental distress—was herself slowly drowning in Alzheimer's disease.

"She was just existing, not living. She was in a nursing home, because it was impossible for us to take care of her at home. It was so depressing to see this wonderful woman, who had been so lively and the hit of every party, look at me and not recognize me. After watching what she went through I'm convinced that it's far, far better to have the pain of cancer than to suffer the hell of Alzheimer's," says Anna. She adds, "It was such a relief when my aunt finally died."

Meanwhile, Anna lost her job. She was simply too depressed to work. She went on welfare and took an under-the-table job taking care of an elderly gentleman in his home. Anna's children were now living on their own—her daughter had even married and gave her a grandchild. Later, when the elderly gentleman had to go to a nursing home,

Anna had to vacate the apartment in his home where she had been living. She moved in with her daughter, son-in-law and three grandchildren.

"I lived with my daughter and her family for two years. Then, on Thanksgiving day, my son-in-law and I had a big fight and I moved out. I stayed with my sister and then with a friend for a few days and then I moved into a rooming house."

* * *

A blonde woman with lively, intelligent blue eyes, Anna is of average height and overweight. She suffers from diabetes, hypertension and arthritis. She takes prescription drugs for each of those illnesses. Yet, she says, she had a difficult time getting a medical card from the welfare office, until her untreated hypertension led to a mild stroke and hospitalization. The County Assistance Office, at her doctor's recommendation, then issued her a retroactive medical card enabling her to pay her hospital bill. Her doctor also declared her disabled and she was able to collect cash benefits—for a while.

Disheartened by the terrible conditions of the rooming house, Anna sought admittance at the Mercy Center For Women on Erie's east side. The facility caters to homeless women without children, and particularly to women recovering from drugs and alcohol. Although Anna did not fit the latter category she was accepted there in December and hoped to live there until she could afford a place of her own.

The Mercy Center is a two-story, five-bedroom house which is beautifully kept by the four women "clients" who live there, along with their manager. Each woman has a bedroom and they share a large kitchen and two bathrooms. Rent for the premises depends on one's ability to pay. Weekly lectures given by guest speakers on subjects such as self-esteem and self-defense are part of the program. Those meetings are mandatory for residents, who otherwise set their own schedules.

In May, Anna saw a sign at the welfare office urging recipients to seek job training at Saint Benedict Education Center. She called Saint Ben's and scheduled an interview. SBEC, it turned out, was housed in her old high school building. She enthusiastically signed up for SBEC's Single Point of Contact (SPOC) program.

Once enrolled in SPOC Anna began to take several courses: reading comprehension, math, typing, medical terminology, and computer, among others. In early October, she excitedly told this writer how happy she was with her course work and the program in general: "I feel very comfortable here, with the nuns, the teachers and even with the other students, although some are much younger than I. If I can afford it, I'd like to get a degree."

By November, however, Anna was not quite so happy. She was abruptly taken off disability sometime in October, leaving her with no income and $135 a month in food stamps. In November she was required to go on a job search; a grant she had been promised by the welfare office and St. Ben's to enable her to buy a car had yet to materialize. She found a job as a telemarketer.

"But because I now had a job I was told I was no longer eligible for the welfare office transportation grant. Yet I need a car to *keep* my job. I leave home at eight in the morning to get to work on time at ten. And even though I leave work at four in the afternoon I don't get home till six in the evening. Why? Because I have to take a bus. So I work six hours a day but spend ten hours going to work, at work, and getting back home."

She continues, "I think there is terrible discrimination in this country against pre-seniors, those of us between the ages of 50 and 64. We get the shaft in everything. We are too young for senior benefits and too old for benefits for those with young children. We are penalized for not having young children. A lot of people didn't plan on being in this situation at this age, but the government doesn't give a damn about that."

Anna, who works six hours a day six days a week at six dollars an hour, says she expects she will soon lose her food stamps, as she is making "too much money." Meanwhile, her employer insists all employees dress "professionally." "That means I have to buy new clothes. The welfare office said I was eligible for $150 for clothing, but how far do you suppose that will go?" To make matters worse, her employer gives points for adherence to the office dress code when evaluating employees for advancement.

And then, her face softening, she says, "I still hope

Sister will help me get a car. I missed school for a couple of days and she didn't like that, but I'm still hopeful and they have been good to me."

POVERTY IS
NO SIN.

Herbert

MOTHERHOOD
by Nancy Small

Motherhood is a precious gift from the Lord
and anyone who experiences it should
feel blessed. Why? Because the Lord picks us
to raise the child, take care of the child,
and be responsible for the child.
The child's growing time will be the years
we'll appreciate once the child is an adult.

These words, taken from an essay on motherhood by Tashara, speak of the two most important things in her life: God and her 14-year-old son Derek. Her deep faith has carried her through many chapters of a difficult life, and motherhood has been central to every step she has taken.

I first met Tashara five months ago at Saint Benedict Education Center where she is enrolled in Community Solutions, a state-funded program that combines a year of job training classes with lessons in life skills such as self-esteem and wellness. At that time, Tashara was receiving cash assistance, food stamps and Medicaid through Temporary Assistance for Needy Families (TANF) and attended SBEC classes from 8:00 a.m. to 4:00 p.m. Monday through Friday. She had just celebrated her 30th birthday. "It's kind of exciting," she said, "because I'm hoping that my next 30 years will be better than my first 30." A quiet smile momentarily eased the half-frown made familiar to her young face by too many years of hardship.

At the tender age of seven, Tashara began playing caretaker to her four younger siblings after her mother and stepfather separated. Her mother, a functional alcoholic, would go out often, and Tashara was left to take care of her three brothers and one sister. Life held little stability as her mother took job after job only to lose each one. They survived on welfare benefits in between jobs.

Tashara developed a fear of her mother that eventually turned into resentment. "I was expected to do everything," she says, "and when I didn't my mother would hit me." When drunk, her mother told Tashara that she was ugly and stupid. When sober, she told her that she loved her. Not knowing what to believe, Tashara's self-esteem suffered greatly. When she began school, she didn't talk much to other people and often remained silent when asked to answer questions in class. "I was afraid they'd treat me like my mother did," she explains. "It was safer to just stay quiet."

As she was growing up, Tashara maintained contact with her step-father whom she describes as a good, stable man. Her birth father has never been a presence in her life. "I feel cheated, in a way," she says. "My brothers and sister know their fathers, but I never had a chance to know mine." Tashara recalls just one time that her father dropped in on her when she was a child. Upon seeing her, the only thing he said was, "Where's your mom?" These words only added to her emptiness.

Through her childhood years, salvation was found in Tashara's grandmother. "If it weren't for my grandmother," she says, "I think I would have ended up a whole lot worse." When her mother's drinking was too much to take, her grandmother was there. When the gas or electricity was shut off or the family faced eviction due to non-payment, her grandmother took them in. And it was her grandmother she ran to after one particularly disturbing argument with her mom at the age of eleven. Recalling the incident, Tashara says, "I decided 'that was it' and I walked out of the house in the middle of winter without a coat, clear across town to my grandmom's house." Determination, one of Tashara's strongest traits, was developed at an early age.

* * *

Becoming a mother helped me to become more responsible as a person. Once I had my son, I had the responsibility of taking care of a person other than myself. I had to be responsible for all his needs and wants, such as food, clothing and shelter. I also had to make time for my son by learning to manage my time between school activities, spending quality time with him, and taking care of his needs.

When she became a mother at sixteen, Tashara made

up her mind that she would still graduate from high school. Not only did she graduate, she made time to participate in the marching band and the business club. "I decided I didn't want to be just a picture with a name under it in my yearbook—I wanted something more."

This motivation to be more has been a driving force in Tashara's life even as she has gone back and forth between jobs and public assistance for the past 10 years. She didn't see how she could manage college with a young son, so she took a job as a kitchen helper in a restaurant shortly after graduation and worked her way up to prep cook. Several years later she worked as a cashier at McDonald's. She left both of these jobs when her son experienced problems with his babysitter and she was unable to find another affordable child care option. During her first time as an adult on public assistance, she voluntarily enrolled in Job Corps training in Washington, DC, making the difficult decision to leave her son in her mother's care while she completed a year's training in business administration.

Returning to Erie with the hope of finding a better job, Tashara applied in numerous places but wasn't hired. "I think it was because of the interviews," she explains. Talking with people she doesn't know and expressing her opinion has been a lifelong difficulty for Tashara. She has been working hard at SBEC on building her self-esteem and speaking out in general. In fact, she has asked all of her teachers to pay attention to her efforts in this area and to let her know when she needs to try harder.

After a year on public assistance and prior to enrolling at SBEC, Tashara was hired as a telephone representative at Teletron. "That was the best job I ever had," says Tashara, "because I worked my way up to $7.50 an hour and had health insurance." Two years into this job, Tashara says she was told by her doctor to stay out of work for a week due to swollen ankles. Her doctor told her he would call Teletron to excuse her from work. A week later, when Tashara returned to work, she was told she had no job. Her boss told her that the doctor had called in a three-day medical excuse, and there was nothing they could do to reinstate her.

At that time, the federal welfare system had been abolished and replaced by TANF, a system that allows individuals a maximum of five years of public assistance. Not wanting to start her TANF clock ticking, Tashara managed to get by without public assistance for about six months. She lost her apartment and began staying with friends. Unable to find work, she finally went back on welfare and stayed in a homeless shelter for four months. "Since I have bad ankles and can't stand a lot, I asked my welfare caseworker to get me into a program that would offer me computer training, and that's how I ended up at SBEC." The welfare office and a community assistance program helped her come up with the money to pay the first month's rent and security deposit on an apartment. The only place that she could afford with her welfare benefits was in a run-down building in a neighborhood known for drug activity where she pays $275 per month. She received used furniture from Family Ties, an organization that assists formerly homeless people.

When I first met her, Tashara's TANF benefits provided her with $316 each month in cash, $234 in food stamps and Medicaid for her and her son. After paying her rent, this left her with only $41 for all other non-food expenses, including utilities. "I'd like to know how the people who decide the cash assistance levels come up with them," she says. "How do they think that two people can live on $316 a month?" She washes most clothes by hand—going to the laundromat is a luxury she can seldom afford. She is unable to afford her utility payments, and she has no phone. "I pay something toward the gas and electric each month, but I can never pay the whole bill," she says. "I figure if I pay something, that might keep them from shutting me off." However, in February Tashara received a shut-off notice for non-payment of her gas bill. She applied for and received emergency fuel assistance, thereby preventing a shut-off. The next month, she received a second shut-off notice. She received emergency assistance again and was set up on a payment plan which requires her to pay her entire monthly fuel bill plus $25 each month toward past-due bills. Speaking to me with a handkerchief covering her head, she told me that her hair had begun to fall out   due to stress.

Although Tashara's son, Derek, is a very big boy for his age and Tashara a large woman, she manages to buy enough food with her food stamps. She knows how to stretch a dollar better than many people, and her pride keeps her away from food pantries or soup kitchens. "I was raised to take care of myself," she says. "It's bad enough having to receive welfare—I just won't go to food pantries or soup kitchens." To stay within her food stamp budget, shopping becomes "an all-day event," traveling to a variety of stores to get the best deals. With no car, Tashara tries to arrange rides from family members for errands like food shopping. Most of the time, she relies on public transportation, which means long bus waits and often several buses to get to her destination.

When Tashara began receiving TANF benefits, her case worker never told her that she was eligible to receive funding to help pay for child care for Derek. Since Tashara was unaware of this benefit, Derek has come home to an empty house since he was 12. Now that he is 14, he is past the age limit for receiving this benefit. "If I could receive funds to pay for child care, I definitely would," Tashara says. "Then I wouldn't have to worry about Derek spending so much time alone."

Outstanding debts are another source of worry. Years ago, Tashara lived in subsidized housing. She was evicted with only a few days' notice because she took in some members of her family in violation of her lease. Unable to find a place to go that quickly, she remained in the apartment for a few days into the following month and was charged the entire month's rent. "I didn't think it was fair to have to pay the whole month's rent when I was only there a few days," she says, "and I needed the money for a new place." Until she pays the money owed, she is unable to live in subsidized housing.

On top of this and the utility bills, there is a $35 outstanding fee for bouncing checks years ago that prevents her from opening a checking account and an outstanding long distance bill from a time when she had a phone and her brother ran up the phone bill unbeknownst to her. An avid reader, she cannot get a library card because she owes money for some library books that were lost when she and Derek were evicted.

* * *

I appreciate my role as a mother more than ever now
because my son is more important to me today.
The time, energy and hard work have all been worth it.
I have turned my son into a fine, mature, young gentleman.
I appreciate the time the Lord has given me with my son,
especially now because he is almost grown. Pretty soon he
will be off to college and into his adult life, and he won't
need to depend on me as much as before.

Despite her hardships, Tashara has given her son something that she never had as a child: the loving care of a mother. "My mother's alcoholism and a sense of responsibility for my son have kept me away from drugs and I only drink occasionally," she says with pride. "I treat my son entirely differently than my mother treated me. Most of the time, I talk to my son when he's misbehaving and I ground him instead of hitting him." Tashara describes her son as well-mannered, with a strong personality and believes that he will go farther in life than she has, but she's quick to add that she plans to go a lot farther. Her son is in the eighth grade, takes some honors classes, plays the trumpet in his school's jazz and concert bands, and plays basketball on his school's team. He is involved in the Boys Club and often goes to events sponsored by Family Ties. Still, Tashara worries about him. "I know that he's strong, but he's exposed to drug deals happening in our neighborhood and the power of peer pressure."

In addition to caring for her son, Tashara has maintained her traditional role as caretaker to the rest of her family. "I'm used to taking care of my family and they're used to it, too," she explains. From the time she began living on her own, family members have come running to her whenever they need help. When they need money for food or other things, they come to Tashara. When her sister ended up in jail for several months, it was Tashara who took care of her sister's children. During that time, Tashara was pregnant with her second child and miscarried at six months. When her mother and siblings have needed somewhere to stay, Tashara has taken them in.

It was during the four months that she spent in a shelter that Tashara realized that the care she gave to her family was not reciprocated. "No one seemed to worry about me being in a shelter," she says. It was then that she resolved to spend more time taking care of herself and less time taking care of her family. Shortly before I first met Tashara, her mother had been staying with her, and she had just decided to tell her mother to leave. "My mother says I'm being selfish," she said. "But I know that if I'm going to get ahead, I need to focus on myself and Derek right now, and that's what I'm going to do. You know," she continued, "once you start being assertive, you look at things a whole lot differently."

* * *

Motherhood has taught me to be responsible for someone other than myself. It has also helped me to mature and appreciate the role it has in my life. Most importantly, it has shown me how important a life is.

In addition to the struggles of her blood relatives, Tashara has also struggled with her relationship to Derek's father, Paul. He and Tashara have been together on and off since before Derek was born. "I know how much it hurts to grow up feeling like your father doesn't want a relationship with you, and I definitely don't want Derek to go through that," she says. And yet, Paul is an alcoholic and addict. He has never paid child support for Derek on a regular basis. He has been on disability at times and working at other times. When working, he has given some money to Tashara to help out. When she lost her apartment and ended up in a shelter, Tashara finally parted ways with Paul. "It's taken me this long to realize that I can't be with him if he's drinking or doing drugs," she says. "It's not good for Derek or for me. I've told him that I love him, but he can only come back if he's clean and working." Tashara recently won her child support case in court and expects to begin receiving $183 per month soon.

In the months that she and Paul have been apart, Tashara has seen a change in Derek. He hasn't been doing his homework consistently like he used to, and he recently received two failing grades. And Tashara has been learning how much of a struggle it is to be a single parent. Paul was in the early stages of recovery when I first met Tashara. Several months later, he was still clean and sober and he and Tashara were talking about getting back together. "I still love him, and he's definitely my best friend," says Tashara. "Nobody knows me like he does."

With so many things to overcome, a person could easily become depressed and discouraged. But not Tashara. "I talk with God all the time," she explains, as if talking about an old friend. "I think he gets tired of talking with me. I know God is everywhere, and I trust that God will guide and uphold me." Tashara is trying her hardest to improve life for herself and Derek. Whenever she can, she spends a day at the public library, reading and improving her computer skills by exploring the internet. Through SBEC, she took courses for her driver's permit and recently took the permit test. Somewhat nervous, she didn't pass the test on her first try. One week later, she returned, determined to pass, and earned a perfect score on her test. Since then, she has made arrangements with friends to practice driving on a regular basis. "I'm hoping that I can get a car and my license by June," she says. Through her program at SBEC, she can receive $750 in TANF funds toward the purchase of a car. "It won't be easy finding a car for $750," she says, "not to mention the registration and insurance."

Her hope of getting a car combined with a growing weariness of trying to make ends meet led Tashara to get a part-time job as a telephone representative recently. She works from 3:30 to 9:00 p.m. three evenings a week and on Saturdays, a total of 22 hours at $6.50 per hour, while still attending more than 30 hours of classes each week. She arranged her work schedule so that she could be home with Derek every other evening. "He doesn't know how to cook too well yet," she says. For the time being, Tashara's sister is helping to look after Derek while Tashara is at work, but it's uncertain how long this will last. She worries about him being left alone, but feels like she has no choice. "We just can't make ends meet on my welfare check," she says.

And now she's struggling to make ends meet with her paycheck. Before taxes, she earns $572 each month. Because of her work income, her TANF cash assistance has been reduced from $316 to $150 each month. Her food stamps were reduced from $234 to $99 during her first |month of work, but she has been told they will go back up to $232. "I had hoped to earn some money to help buy a car, but so far I haven't been able to save anything."

Before she began her new job, she and I went clothes shopping, using the $150 clothing allowance granted to TANF recipients when they find a job. Tashara knew exactly where to go to get the best deals, and I was amazed at how much she was able to buy and still stay within the $150 allowance. "This is the first time I've bought clothes for myself in years, " she said. Her quiet excitement was evident.

The view that our society often has of people who receive public assistance is well known to Tashara, and she wonders why anyone would think that people are content to remain on welfare. "Being on welfare is hard," she says, "really, really hard. You never have enough money to cover your basic needs, never mind things you want. People look at you like you're lazy when they see you use food stamps or your Access (welfare benefits) card. They have a set idea in their mind of what a person on welfare is like. And I certainly am not like the kind of person they have in mind."

Being on welfare can also be a barrier to getting back on your feet, she believes. "Sometimes you wonder if you'll ever break out of the welfare cycle." She has grown to hate the word "welfare." "It's such an ugly word," she says. "I want to be so far away from that word that I never hear it again."

Welfare benefits and, therefore, the lives of people on welfare could be improved if those making decisions would only sit down and listen to people who are trying to live on welfare, Tashara believes. She's not convinced that those who are making decisions about people on welfare really have the best interests of the people in mind. "If they do, then why are there so many needs that aren't addressed? Why don't they ask us what we need and take that into consideration? Everyone that I know who is on welfare is trying to get off of it, but we keep hitting roadblocks." It's the roadblocks—things like transportation and child care—that welfare policy makers should be focusing on, she believes, rather than quick-fix methods for moving people off of welfare.

Nearing the end of her SBEC program, Tashara believes she is closer to finding a good job. SBEC has helped her to work on her self-esteem. She knows much more about computers than she ever did. She has improved her English and typing skills, and she has learned medical terminology that might help her to become a medical assistant. In August, she will finish her classwork at SBEC and the difficult work of finding a job with a living wage will begin. A job developer at SBEC will assist her with this and her case manager will stay in touch with her for the next year to offer assistance. By December, she will need to be in a work activity for a minimum of 20 hours a week if she wants to receive any TANF benefits at all. She is hoping that her Medicaid benefits will continue, at least for her son, once she begins working full-time.

Tashara has many qualities essential to success. She is hardworking, independent, a fast learner, dependable, punctual, determined, friendly, easy-going, intelligent and resourceful. Her struggle with self-esteem is perhaps the greatest challenge she faces. On the one hand, she is a very smart, courageous woman who knows that she can succeed. And on the other, she is the child who was raised believing she isn't good enough.

Looking back on all the hardships she has survived is one way that Tashara is learning to recognize her potential and to believe that she has what it takes to be successful. "Sister Mary Louis says it's like the caterpillar and the butterfly," she explains. "In the past, I was like the caterpillar that is unfinished. Now I'm trying to improve myself, like I'm going through the cocoon stage. I'm starting to blossom into a beautiful butterfly."

A butterfly that dreams. She thinks about going to college one day, probably after Derek goes himself. She dreams of owning her own company, maybe one that would offer attractive clothing for larger women like herself. She would like to have one more child, hopefully a girl, "but not until I get my life back together." And she dreams of owning her own house, maybe by the time she's 35. "I don't want anything fancy," she says, "just something that is small, cuddly and cute. Something big enough for my family to come visit, but not big enough for them to stay."

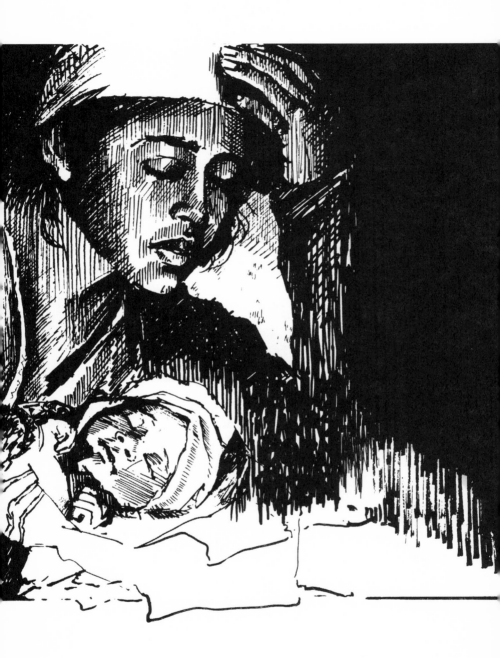

THAT'S OUR TASK:
NOT TO ROMANTICIZE THE POOR
BUT TO PERSONALIZE THE POOR.

Joan Chittister, OSB

EPILOGUE
by Joan Chittister, OSB

"Any solution to a problem," R.W. Johnson wrote, "changes the problem." Having finally recognized the problem of poverty in the United States, we now have a new one. We know now that welfare checks are not the only answer to poverty. On the contrary, we have come to decide they may actually cause it. We obviously need a great deal more than that, but what?

Poverty is not only a misfortune, it is a scandal in a country plump with a burgeoning stock exchange and nursed on a philosophy of rugged individualism—the notion that anyone who is ambitious enough and scrappy enough and determined enough to succeed can succeed. In that kind of social climate, the poor are not simply ignored, they are despised. They are painted as shiftless and pathetic creatures who prefer the dregs of life to its heights.

The picture is not completely untrue, of course. There are those who are in poverty because they made choices that plunged them into a life mired in drink and drugs and dirty living conditions from which they are unable or unwilling to escape, for whatever reasons.

There is another kind of poverty, however, that has

nothing whatsoever to do with qualities of personal choice. This species of deprivation comes from being born into a poverty from which there is no escape; no one in the family who can read to you when you are just discovering that learning to read is difficult; no educational climate to prepare you for college or technical school, no idea even that you should go; no parents to fall back on for a loan when, later, the chance comes to buy the car that will enable you to commute to your first real job; no emotional support to carry you through the natural disasters of the lost first job or the first loan or the increase in rent and the cuts in salary and work hours because no one in your family has ever even gotten that far, let alone survived it.

There is simply no history of family success to lead you to your own star to steer by. There is often little or no family at all: just a collection of adults going from job to job, from place to place, from system to system in a world in which they can never, ever get ahead because no one will hire them, or no one will pay them a just wage, or no one will allow them to save an extra cent without threatening to take their food stamps away.

To romanticize the poor, to glorify "the simple life," is to do these people, as well as ourselves, irreparable damage. When we can convince ourselves that the poor are really happy that way—without the hot water and heat and couches and beds and kitchenware that we take for granted—we give ourselves the right to disenfranchise whole segments of the population from the standards of humanity we claim for ourselves. When we idealize the poor as fonts of simple wisdom who have no need for continued personal development, we deny a whole class of society the right to bring their wisdom to the public arena. When we assume that the poor are simply born that way and can choose to leave it any time they want to, we ignore the implications of a rapidly expanding technological society in which lies the specter of a quickly emerging permanent underclass—too limited, too undereducated, to do more than flip the hamburgers or wait the tables of a permanent upper class who hire them only part time and afford them no benefits. When we assume that the poor are meant to be poor, we diminish the idea of a great, generous, gratuitous God.

Indeed, when we argue that the poor want to be poor, it excuses us the long, hard task of understanding the problem so that we can deal with it for all our sakes. It fails to explain, for instance, why so many of the poor do not succeed, even when structures seem to be in place to help them. It fails to apprehend the legacy of poverty as it is passed from one generation to another. It declines to recognize that poverty is a social blight that affects the stable as well as the financially insecure, the comfortable as well as the destitute by turning sectors of every city into drug havens where the pain of one problem is drowned by the mind-stealing trap of another problem. It takes the rest of us out of the picture and so leaves the picture of the rends in our social fabric incomplete.

This book, *Breaking the Cycle of Indignity: Welfare Reform Face-to-Face,* took us into the personal lives of poor women who lived in the dregs of poverty, fell back into it again and again, and then, finally, with the proper care, with help from the right people, with a kind of attention that enabled them to see themselves as worthy, became worthy of respect in the eyes of other people, as well. "It's a fine thing to rise above pride," George Bernanos wrote, "but you must have pride in order to do so."

The desperately poor, the people who do not have three meals a day, who cannot find steady work because they can't do the simplest of sums, write the most basic of letters, read the most elementary of sentences, need first to value themselves and then to be valued by others before they can possibly assume to do anything valuable for the rest of society.

That's our task: not to romanticize the poor but to personalize the poor. It requires that we get to know them as human beings, one at a time, up close and personal. It insists that we understand what they inherited from the poor generation before them and why. It makes us understand how it is that their poverty is actually a reflection, a symptom, a barometer of our own.

We need more books like *Breaking the Cycle of Indignity.* We need to get to know the poor face-to-face as the staff at Saint Benedict Education Center knows them, to recognize in them what could have happened to our own children, to our own lives if we had been born into as little as they were. We need to learn from them what it was in this program that really helped them break the cycle of indignity and then we must do more of it. We need to listen to what they tell us they need now if they are to complete the transition from the poverty we abhor in them to the personhood of which they are clearly capable. We need to discover what it is that still needs to be done if we are to be a country where life is really valued and a nation where the future is safe from the kind of degradation that leads to a population of angry poor standing at the guardhouses of our gated communities. John F. Kennedy, in his inaugural address of January 1961 said, "If a free society cannot help the many who are poor, it cannot save the few who are rich." It is a prophecy the kind of which can only be escaped when we take hands, one with another, rich with poor, to make this a nation where poverty may be chosen but never imposed.

—Updates on the Stories

Due to the length of time between the interviews for this book and the time the book was ready to be sent to the publisher, a number of new developments occurred in the lives of the women. About one month before the final document was sent to the printer, we made contact with each woman to get an update as to what has happened since the stories were written.

ATISHA (page 18)

Atisha returned to SBEC prior to the publication of this book. She was referred to SBEC by the County Assistance Office because she was back on cash assistance and needed to enroll in a Welfare-to-Work initiative. Atisha explained that since the last time we talked, she lost her job. Unfortunately, the lack of employment created an avalanche of other problems. She could no longer afford to pay her rent so she was evicted and lost her housing. Since moving out of her own home, she has been staying with various friends and family members, moving her belongings and her children when things make it difficult to stay. This in turn has effected her ability to get a job. Atisha said that not having a stable residence makes it hard to apply and interview for jobs.

Another problem related to her lack of housing involves getting her children to school. She used to live right near the elementary school. Now, proximity to the school is not a priority so when the children go to school Atisha has to get them up at 6:30 a.m. in order to walk to the school from different parts of the city. She said she does not have any extra money for them to take the city bus and since they move around it is hard to arrange for the school bus to transport them. In addition, she had to sell her car and return to cash assistance and food stamps. Atisha said that she does want to work again and she admitted that the reason she lost her job was not the employer's fault, she wanted to "hang out" and party with her friends who do not work.

NIKISHA (page 33)

Nikisha did not quit. She was placed in an employment situation that she enjoys and values. And, fortunately the relationship is mutual; the employer is very pleased with Nikisha. She is proud that both of her children are doing well and they are both on the school honor roll. She explained that she is still dealing with the murder of her family member. Nikisha has attended all of the court hearings and trials related to the murder. Nikisha says that the pain has eased with time, her family is doing better and they will be okay. Her face brightened considerably when she shared that she bought a new car and her next goal is to become a homeowner.

BETTY (page 42)

Betty did come to SBEC to read her story before the book was sent to the publisher but she chose not to share an update of her current situation.

NICOLE (page 61)

After much deliberation, Nicole decided to quit her job in order to devote more time to working towards her Bachelor's Degree in Social Work and Criminal Justice. In order to go to school full-time, Nicole has relied on grants, loans, her part-time job at the University and the understanding of her significant other. Nicole is doing well as a full-time student and she plans to graduate in a year and a half. Nicole also says that her two sons are doing very well.

SHONDA (page 70)

Every so often people who work in social services are presented with unexpected visits that make their day. Shonda comes to SBEC periodically to let us know how she is doing and to offer her appreciation for our assistance—it makes our day! Pursuing her GED and getting a driver's license had been top priorities for Shonda. With SBEC's help she achieved both of these goals since her story was written. She is delighted and shares how proud she is of these achievements. Shonda continues to be clean and sober. She is employed and also persists in her search for upgraded employment and is making healthy strides toward self-sufficiency.

LUCY (page 79)
Lucy remains with the same employer mentioned in her story and is doing very well there. After putting in many service hours, Lucy and her two children moved into a Habitat for Humanity home. Lucy is thrilled! In an effort to continue to improve herself and her abilities, Lucy enrolled in another welfare initiative to assist with job retention and advancement.

ANNA (page 88)
After leaving SBEC, Anna continued to work as a telemarketer for a time and the program at 9.5 assisted her in purchasing a car. Striving to gain upgraded employment led Anna to a medical internship at a local hospital. She did exceptionally well and upon completion of the program was hired in a doctor's office. Unfortunately, due to a contract disagreement, Anna was let go from her job. Now unemployed, she is applying for medical disability due to severe knee pain. Funds to access life sustaining prescription medication continue to be a desperate struggle. Although things are difficult, the light of Anna's life is the relationship she enjoys with her family, including her children and grandchildren.

TASHARA (page 97)
Tashara completed the program and gained full-time employment. Once employed, she was able to get help with housing through Dwelling and Advocacy for Women in Need (Erie DAWN). Once she was in stable and safe housing, she enrolled in a SBEC welfare initiative to assist her with job advancement and retention. Within a short period of time, Tashara was hired at a community agency and earned an increased wage. Because a car was needed for employment, the program helped Tashara

purchase a used car. Unfortunately, she did not make it through her probation time and lost the job. Tashara continued to push forward and is again employed. She is proud of her son who continues to do well in school; he is looking towards going to college after graduation. Tashara wants to work full-time and she continues to persevere in the labor force.

—Update on Welfare Employment and Training Programs

The Pennsylvania Department of Public Welfare (DPW), Bureau of Employment and Training Programs, is to be commended for the continuing assessment of the effectiveness of programs operated under their auspices and meaningful program adjustments made in the light of the assessments.

Though bound in many instances by federa welfare policies, the Bureau works diligently to provide assistance and services which help remove welfare recipient barriers to employment and which help ensure job retention for employed individuals.

Since these stories were written, DPW has implemented a new initiative designed to help the "working poor" persist and advance in employment. The Job Retention, Advancement, and Rapid Re-Employment Program provides intensive case management, additional job training, and a number of supportive services for underemployed working parents.

—About the authors

Joan Chittister, OSB
is an international lecturer and author. She crisscrosses the globe addressing issues concerning women, justice, spirituality and Benedictinism. A member of the Benedictine Sisters of Erie, Sister Joan is the Executive Director of Benetvision: Research and Resources for Contemporary Spirituality. A prolific author, Sister Joan's latest books include *Illuminated Life: Monastic Wisdom for Seekers of Light* (Orbis), *The Story of Ruth: Twelve Moments in Every Woman's Life* (Wm. B. Eerdmans Publishing Co.) and *The Friendship of Women: A Spiritual Tradition* (Benetvision).

Mary Amthor
is a high school German/History teacher at Erie's Northwest Pennsylvania Collegiate Academy after a first career as a journalist. She spent 10 years in Europe working for varous news organizations before anchoring the 11 o'clock News on Erie's CBS Channel 35, WSEE, for two years. Assignments and travel have taken her to some 30 different countries.

Julie Cullen
is an Erie native who graduated from John Carroll University with a B.A. in English. She recently graduated from Mercyhurst College, Erie, PA, with a master's degree in the Administration of Criminal Justice.

Edwina Gateley
is the founder of the Volunteer Missionary Movement in England, Genesis House, a house of hospitality for women involved in prostitution, in Chicago and Exodus, a support program for graduates of Genesis House. Edwina is internationally recognized as a poet, writer and lecturer. Her published works include ten books and numerous audio tapes and articles.

Mary Hembrow Snyder, PhD

is a Professor of Religious Studies at Mercyhurst College in Erie, PA where she is also the Director of the Department of Philosophy and Religious Studies. Her most recent publication is the *festschrift* she edited, *Spiritual Questions for the Twenty-First Century: Essays in Honor of Joan D. Chittister* (Orbis Books, 2001).

Mukami Ireri

is a journalist and writer whose work has been published in *The New York Times* and *ESSENCE*, among other publications. She currently lives and writes in Erie, PA, where she also teaches creative writing at the Inner-City Neighborhood Art House.

Holly Knight

is director of communications and public relations for the Sisters, Servants of the Immaculate Heart of Mary in Monroe, Michigan. She is former director of communications for Pax Christi, USA, the national Catholic peace movement. She has been published in *Creation Spirituality Magazine, Community Journal, The Mount, The Antiochian* and other periodicals.

Marie Quinn

currently serves as job readiness coordinator and teacher in employment and training programs at St. Benedict Education Center. She has worked at SBEC for over twelve years. Marie has also taught art, co-authored art education grants, written extensively for the business community, and designed a self-discovery imaging process for counselors and teachers.

Nancy Small

is the former national coordinator of Pax Christi, USA, the national Catholic peace movement. She has written numerous articles on various peace and justice issues and the spirituality of nonviolence. She speaks to groups throughout the US on these topics

—About the artist

Helen David Brancato, IHM
is the art center director at the Southwest Community Enrichment Center in Philadelphia. Helen David has illustrated a number of books including *Walk with Jesus* by Henri J.M. Nouwen and *Why Not Become Fire? Encounters with Women Mystics* by Evelyn Mattern.